IN THAT MILL, I TOO WAS FORGED

IN THAT MILL, I TOO WAS FORGED

✦POEMS✦

NARAYAN SURVE

Translated by

JERRY PINTO

SPEAKING TIGER

SPEAKING TIGER BOOKS LLP
125A, Ground Floor, Shahpur Jat, near Asiad Village,
New Delhi 110049

First published by Speaking Tiger in 2023

ISBN: 978-93-5447-640-2
eISBN: 978-93-5447-642-6

10 9 8 7 6 5 4 3 2 1

Typeset in Baskerville MT Std by SÜRYA, New Delhi
Printed at Chaman Enterprises, New Delhi

CONTENTS

Narayan Surve, the people's poet

Translator's note

I did not think much of poetry as a child. The queen had often lost her thimble and a solitary reaper sang about her bunions (for all the poet knew). We studied poetry in two other languages too, Marathi and Hindi, and they were full of cheery postmen who delivered letters and girls who wanted to tie raakhis on their brothers' wrists. We learned them all by rote and reduced stanzas to paragraphs of prose. Nothing spoke to me.

Then in the tenth standard, I read 'Futility' by Wilfred Owen and my attitude to poetry changed forever. I wanted to be able to do this, to make a boy I would never know in another country, in another time, weep over the criminal waste of a young life. Only, I had not been to war, and with my poor eyesight, I knew (with a guilty feeling of relief) that I would never hear the stuttering rifles pattering out their hasty orisons myself. I could not give myself permission to write poetry without that, I thought. If this sounds daft, you must remember I was fourteen.

I first saw Narayan Surve on stage at the National Centre for the Performing Arts. It was a multilingual poetry reading and there is often nothing so well-intentioned. But then Mr Surve got up to read and there it was again, an odd familiar surge. The desire to be able to make poetry like this: direct, appealing, raw. I wanted to do to language what Narayan Surve did to it that evening. I heard familiar words being mauled in the way I had heard them mauled on the bus and on the train. I heard in it the voices of the many people he said he had inside his head. I heard another kind of poetry, a city poetry, a poetry of mill and marching, a poetry of hard-working women and men hard-pressed.

And again I felt a terrible feeling. I would never live his life. I would never be a millworker, a doffer boy, a peon, a municipal school teacher.

Why am I telling you all this? I'm trying to explain how I got to translate him. And I'm taking a page out of Surve's introduction to his poetry, first published in a collection in 1982. It is rare to have such a mapping of a poet's journey told in his own words. In it, he declares clearly that he has had to construct a self, perhaps in the absence of other markers. I believe that we all do; a self doesn't just happen to you along the way. Each choice positions you here or there. Each person you meet changes you in some way. Each book you read shapes your voice. And your voice is also something you can choose and you can construct. Much of this is only visible in hindsight and that is always clouded over by nostalgia and self-exculpation, but it makes a nice change from the somewhat self-congratulatory tone in which poets talk about poets being shamans, mystics and sages. (A poet might become all of the above but only in the way a poem interacts with a reader. But most of all, it cannot be a self-appointment.)

Thus, for me, the introduction Surve wrote is also an important part of this book. It is partly autobiographical but it is also autographical—and it is written without any self-congratulation, although there is a trace of forgivable glee when Surve, rejected by the establishment on many counts, finds himself part of the awards committee, the textbook committee and so on.

I read Surve with thirst, with greed. When Naresh Fernandes was going to meet him—he was working on an essay on the great mill strike of 1982 for *India* magazine, which we would later include in *Bombay, Meri Jaan: Writings on Mumbai*, an anthology we worked on for Ravi Singh when he was at Penguin India—he asked if I would like to come along. I did not go. I think it was because I was so much in awe of the man I had seen on the stage, I did not want to risk meeting him in person and being disappointed; perhaps Eunice de Souza's 'better to meet in poems' was in my ears. It is one of my greatest regrets.

I did meet him a little later, when Shanta Gokhale was writing a script for the documentary that was eventually to become the wonderful *Narayan Gangaram Surve* (Arun Khopkar, 2002).

'The Surve film began with me,' Gokhale told me when I was interviewing her for this book. 'I remember Surve and I were both at some conference or meeting or event—I've forgotten what—at the Yashwantrao Chavan

Centre and we were walking down the road, past the ministers' cottages at Nariman Point. Up ahead, there were four or five men, obviously of the working class. They saw Surve and their faces lit up with huge smiles. They came up and talked to him, greeting him without obsequiousness. And he too responded, patting one on the back, chatting naturally and spontaneously. Into my mind came the phrase: the people's poet.'

I did drop in this time but it was in the middle of the shooting and there wasn't much time to talk. So I did the next best thing. I translated him. I'm not going to tell you tales of the losses of translation: they bore me. I believe that the gains in translation far outweigh the losses. If we did not have translations, what would we know of Akhmatova, Basho, Cavafy, Dnyaneshwar, Eknath, Fuzuli, Guillevic, Popati Hiranandani, Ibopishak, Juvenal, Koziol, Lalleshwari, Muktibodh, Neruda, Oberg, Pessoa, Qabbani, Rengetsu, Szymborska, Transtromer, Ungaretti, Mahadevi Varma, Cai Wenji, Xu Zhimo, Yevtushenko, Zanzotto...make your own list and recite it every time someone brings out that old shibboleth.

I enjoyed the challenge of the spoken voice, of the unselfconscious segue between Marathi and Hindi and dialects thereof. This has nothing to do with 'language'; it has to do with how people speak, how any big city dweller sees language as a huge box of tools. This is how language lives in Mumbai, Bombay, Bambai, Momoi, Mhamai, and how we speak, moving from one to another, crafting our language, our dialect, our multi-tongued, polyrhythmic, many-hued boli. We have been shamed for it by purists of many stripes. We have often been ashamed of it; we should celebrate it. Surve shows us how. It is therefore our great modern tragedy that our cities are turning into linguistic battlefields; in this too my city has shown the way.

When language lives and works without political expedience, when it is off-stage and off-centre, it offers itself up for our use: I am vella today is not the same as I am idle today and it is not the same as I am lukkha. A translator may have to worry about the distinction between these, the subtle shades of difference. The poet who chooses to reflect the polyphony of his city has access, unlimited access. And in Surve's poetry, we are granted access to another world, one not so very far away from our own. (At least, it wasn't in Bombay where you could walk down a street and watch it turn from middle-class to working-class in a building or two.) This is the world of labour, where no one minds doing a hard day's work. In the rhythms of 'Song of the mill', you can see pride and joy at the work they do. Being a textile mill worker brought Surve close to Sant Kabir and to Lord Krishna; I leave you to discover how. Being a teacher in a municipal school taught him how to be a poet; again, I will let you read on and discover for yourself. What angers Surve is the fact that it is so difficult to make a living out of that labour. The farmer, the doffer boy and the sex worker whom we meet in these pages bring a certain pride to what they do; they can't forgive the inequity that breaks their backs to keep the bourgeois happy.

The bourgeois? That would include my kind and my class, if biology and biography is destiny. (If you want to debate this, perhaps you might want to talk to someone who was abandoned on a rubbish heap as a baby.) The discomfort of my identity vis-a-vis these poems, these translations, was offset by the tone of the poems. They did not, I felt, seek to discomfit me. They stated what the poet saw and if the reader sees truth in those lines, uncomfortable truths, it is for the reader to own that response. Surve's voice is inclusive and accepting of all the variations of identity that may be shaped and served up by the city. It is a voice to which I was drawn because of the natural speaking voice, the tone of the poems, the banked fires in them, the refusal to lose hope and by the fact that there is so little poetry like this around, even decades after Surve first raised his voice with 'My field on the hill'.

I loved the mountains he forced me to climb in 'My university' and 'Mumbai'. I loved the easy way he initiates a conversation with B.S. Mardhekar, poet, aesthete and literary revolutionary. The idea of Surve and Mardhekar sitting on a kerb and disrupting the hierarchies of Girgaon—a Brahmin enclave—and Girangaon—a working-class locality—is delightful. Marx turns up at a gate meeting and asks after Surve's 'poetry-shoetry'. Surve poses a lively and vivid challenge to the Saraswat (read Brahmin) stranglehold over Marathi but hidden in that poem is a vibrant warning too. His sins may be venial, as he puts it, but he also can write: I burn my brand into your door.

Surve dares. Oh yes, Surve dares. And with that daring, he became a flaming sword. It was a sword he would turn against hypocrisy, communal feeling, but he was also a critic of the Party to which he belonged. He was never disillusioned by Marxism in theory; he wasn't always happy with how it was practised. And what was important was that he never hesitated to speak out against it.

Surve may no longer be with us, but his words have been released into the world; they are still powerful. I love the poem in which he tells his wife to stand firm; Krishnabai, you will see, from her interventions in the interview, was a doughty warrior, a fellow marcher, a born protester. But Surve was not writing for her alone; he was writing for all those who love a flaming sword and must watch as it goes out into the night to meet with its destiny.

To all those who need it, then, and honestly, I often need it too: *Tharku naka.* Stand firm.

JERRY PINTO

Mahim (where Surve spent his growing-up years)

'What I saw, I wrote'

The poet's introduction

I was born an orphan. This is a sad thing. It is also the unadorned truth. Even as I write this, hundreds of desperate mothers, for whom all options have been closed, are abandoning their children in hospitals, on the streets, in the fields and forests. What they feel at that moment, we can only gauge by logical reasoning. When the mother who gave me life cut the umbilical cord and gave me up for good, did she feel as if her world were coming to an end? Did she tremble as a flame in a storm? Did she feel a frenzy of shame? If a woman is unhappy about being pregnant, there is no greater curse than bearing a child. What my mother did after she abandoned me, only she knows.

Anyway, fate seems to have had other plans for me. If someone had not taken pity on me and adopted me, I should not be here. But that did not happen. There is a store of humanity in all of us. One woman may have cut the cord that bound me to her but another took me to her bosom. This is my second mother, a force greater in my life than she who gave me life. Had she not been a formidable person, she would not have taken an orphan as her own. She brought me up, cleaned my shit and piss, and made me hers. In this huge world, she bound us together, with an umbilicus of her own making. I had no name, but when I am no longer here, I will leave one behind: Narayan Gangaram Surve.

The couple who gave me this name came from a working-class family. I say this with pride for I believe it is something to say with pride. I now belonged to one of Mumbai's many proud revolutionary worker families. They lived by the sweat of their labour. My father, Shri Gangaram Kushaji Surve, worked in the spinning department of the India Woollen Mills, Mumbai; and my mother, Kashibai, was in the binding department of the Kamala Mills. Both were mill workers. On the eve of Dassehra, the mill workers decorate their machines. Everything is festooned with buntings, garlands made out of flowers, balloons and flags. The entire department is decked up. That day, Aai would set me and my sister, Sakhu, each on one hip, and take us to her workplace. I would have a new shirt and a new cap embroidered with gold thread. We'd spend a little time at her department and then a great deal of time at the mill where our father worked. I was very young when I was introduced to the various sections of the mill—the spinning department, the binding department and the accounts. I was being moulded. In the poem, 'Mumbai', I wrote about this:

> Ever since I can recall, I took him his bhakri and pickle.
> In that mill, I too was forged, as a blacksmith does a sickle.
>
> I learned to string cotton, to fit spindle to socket just right.
> And in good time, I learned to down tools to fight the good fight.

Just as the ironsmith heats iron in the thundering fires of a furnace and shapes it, I was being formed. I kept my ears, my eyes and my mind open, and absorbed everything. This was my school. I lived on a small spit of Mumbai's land but I got to see the entire world in the microcosm of those departments.

From the Sahyadris they came, these men, half-farmers still, in search of work to fill their stomachs—and the number of their settlements grew apace. Money orders from Mumbai would help keep the home fires burning in the Konkan. And so it is to this day. Only, at that time, the majority of the Mumbai mill workers were from the Konkan. After the Quit India Movement of 1942, large numbers began to come to Mumbai from the Desh area, the Deccan Plateau region of west-central Maharashtra. It had always been a productive area, but on account of the global recession and the World War, able-bodied men began to come to the city. Psychologically speaking, though, these men never managed to snap ties with the village. They were still bound to the soil. Their villages were alive and well in their hearts. After 1960, this class, whom we can refer to as the proletariat, became the real backbone of the city; it was upon their labour that the city depended, the mills, the factories, the showrooms, all of it. And their numbers grew.

In the old days, the textile mills were the most important businesses. The major unions were the mill worker unions. Today, the picture has changed. Different businesses and industries—banks and insurance companies, for instance—came into existence, bringing different languages with them; now we have technical workers and unskilled labourers, transport workers, intellectual workers. Some sell the work of their brain, some sell the labour of their bodies—but all of them are selling their labour. How to get these workers to unite in the struggle against political and economic exploitation is the new challenge. I can see a new leader in this battlefield in the war against exploitation. He comes from a class that was deeply exploited and full of unhappiness. But he believes in a better tomorrow.

~

Every morning, my father would set out to work on foot. My mother too. My father would return when it was night, my mother in the evening. Everyone walked to and from work. Kerosene lamps lit our homes in the night. Aai would light the firewood, blowing on the sticks with a pipe bellows that was placed above the stove. Work shifts lasted for twelve exhausting hours. There were no rules. The trade unions were fighting for eight-hour shifts. Slogans, handbills and meetings, these were the means with which they spread awareness.

The clouds of war hovered above us. Gandhi, Nehru and Dange* were discussed widely at home and outside.

---

* Comrade Shripad Amrit Dange (1889–1991) was a member of the Communist Party of India and a stalwart of the trade union movement in India.

These three great leaders were always being talked about but I could not tell the difference between their political and theoretical positions. Pandit Jawaharlal Nehru made the demand for Total Independence and also announced that the nation should be given a socialist framework. This caused tumult among the administrators of the British Raj. Mahatma Gandhi spoke in a gentler voice, but after 1942, he got a lot tougher. Comrade Dange had the ear of the workers. The struggle for independence was becoming more focused and there was a call for the Communists and the Socialists and their trade unions to take active part in it.

The workers' movement included men and women of all faiths, castes and communities. Every stratum of society that faced exploitation, whether it was political, social, economic, cultural or psychological, took part in the movement. It was led by ordinary people. There was a general understanding that workers had no caste and no class differences, or such was the feeling.

This is what we see in the broader freedom movement as well. In it too, it was a general item of belief that it was necessary to first throw off the yoke of British oppression. Once we were independent, we would find ourselves in Utopia! Or so we believed. Even so, it was not that the question of caste and class did not exist. The terrible caste riots that took place in that period are proof of this. The Chavdar Tank agitation and other incidents of that kind would keep happening.

I write all this because our nation was going through a time of tumult and change, rich with energy and excitement, as if we were faced with a series of ultimatums. All this was reflected in the workers' lives both inside and outside the factory. When we got up in the morning and walked down the streets, the slogans we had chalked on the walls or the posters that had been pasted at night served as information. The posters and the walls were the newspapers of the working class. They were also a barometer. They told us what was happening and what ought to happen. The government paid as much attention to the workers' movement as it did to the independence struggle.

I put sorrow behind me; I was growing up in a militant atmosphere. The environment was such that one had to fight passionately for one's rights, one's independence. In general, most enlightened workers were members of some union or the other. Both my father and mother were members of the Girni Kamgar Union. You could see the influence of the unions in their everyday speech. There were discussions about how one might run a strike for six months or more, and they would gleefully explain how best to break the legs of scabs (those who tried to break strikes).

Being an adopted child meant that people would feel a little sorry for me. If I went to Aai's binding department with her lunch box, her fellow workers would send out something for me to eat.

Those who have nothing but the work of their hands can have huge hearts; this was demonstrated again and again. The women workers of the mills brought an intense, stubborn, militant energy to the workers' movement. At that time, women workers in the accounts department would do their hair differently—'*pankhe kaadi*' it was called, which meant that a lock of hair, like a feather, would be drawn out to fall across the forehead. That was the working-class fashion of those times and if the woman were a muqaddam [the equivalent of a foreman], she was certain to do her hair in this manner. There might be flecks of cotton all over their hair but an ear ornament would nestle there too.

I observed the people around, studying them and their mannerisms in detail. In times of grief, they would be bewildered or fearful, but in a few minutes, they would recover. Because this was a world of people who lived by selling their labour, there was unity, a willingness to understand, peace and friendship. You would always have someone to celebrate with you and four willing sets of shoulders would present themselves when needed. For my people knew how to share sorrow; they made of it a useful habit. And since they lived almost as a clan, they could partake of each other's joys and sorrows; nor did they fear a fight. These areas were like a beehive; but you could only belong by virtue of labour, and if in any of these areas bulldozers were brought in, the clan would come together to fight them with as much intensity as they could muster.

Resistance—the word itself was a slogan here. Hundreds of martyrs offered their lives for the country. The workers in these areas were productive but also conscious of what was going on around them.

> I have no words to tell of the courage here, Bappa.
> All those who write should drink deep of this spring.

These lines I wrote are not to be found in any of the three collections I have published. But I have included them here because I felt I should. Theirs was a way of life that demanded change and demanded it aggressively.

My nature drew me to the Communist movement and this proved to be an association of great importance to me. The benefit of this was that instead of a caste-based movement or one that was all smoke and mirrors, I got bound to a scientific and universal movement. It gave me from the very beginning the basic scientific understanding that you have to change the interior landscape before you change the world outside, that it is the community that counts but the individual that is paramount. This philosophy was much more eye-opening to me than all the scriptures and texts of the pundits. Its name was Marxism-Leninism. It was with this third eye that I moved forward. It helped me confront reality as it exists, to make use of the understanding I had developed, to turn experiences into questions, and to use these to change myself into an activist who could engage with the world and would also help the other person change. Truly, it is important to have clarity in one's thought process.

Just as it is important to have a strong spine to stand firm, so it is with one's thinking. To stumble along, saying that one does not believe in any political or philosophical system, to claim even that one is above such systems, but then to ask people to change while looking down upon them, is to fool oneself and to set oneself up for failure. But this pretence continues...to keep other people in a condition of slavery.

Artists and activists must give witness, they must stand tall with torches in their hands. For what does art mean? It is a truth brewed in the still of life; or derived in the beakers and retorts of life's chemical reactions. Thought is no different. History demonstrates that our creations exist in a social context.

For the litterateur to break up literature and philosophy into separate units, and after having so divided them, to give them different positions in a hierarchy, or to use their thought bases merely for debate, is to take the position of the blind men of the Mahanubhavis. In the analyses others have made of what I have written, I keep seeing this in action and it makes me laugh.

Even as all the struggles of life—a job, a home, a place to stay—were on, so also and perhaps even a little more, I was trying to understand what was happening around and to me, in order to become an enlightened activist.

I had only studied up to the fourth standard. Such an education had not much value or meaning in practical terms. I had no caste, no religion and no relatives to stand by me. In this country, if you want to walk with your head held high, you must have at least one of the above as support. They are legacies we are all supposed to have. This is unfortunate. But it is what it is. It is not of much use but sometimes a drowning man will clutch at a straw. I can tell you many such stories. I went through many unpleasant experiences because of this.

But one good thing came of it: since I had neither caste nor religion, I had nothing to lose. In fact, it benefited me. I began to see humanity as a single caste. In 'My university', I wrote:

> I met men of every stripe: brothers, fathers, exploiters some.
> I seared my soul on a tarry griddle, baked by a relentless sun.
> The endless inventiveness of humankind impresses me.
> With thirty-seven pages of my story done, how little I've seen depresses me.

I encountered creative minds everywhere, as much among the activists and workers as among the scholars, and certainly among all the people I loved. If one keeps the doors of one's mental storehouse wide open, what experiences one can have! I stored these up with the greatest care.

This is a world in which millions of people live. Or they just survive. Nothing wrong in that. But those who have a sustaining vision become activists. These are restless souls. They want to build something. They have something to say, something to create. I felt this too.

I wanted to say something. I wanted to write something. And so I turned to poetry. But before that I began writing stories. I also translated some Hindi stories and published them, stories that agreed with my worldview. I even wrote some letters that were published in the newspaper *Nav Shakti*. This was my apprenticeship in the workshop of the word. I was trying my hand; checking whether I could write or not; checking whether what I wrote would be seen as worthy of being published. I had not sat for even a single examination in Hindi or Urdu. I was in the thick of a people's movement. I used that as my material. I gave it shape in language. And since I dug deep within myself to do this, it brought me a great deal of satisfaction.

I began to educate myself through my own experiences. I was thc author and the first reader of my own writing. I would read each piece ten times and then tear it up and ask myself why I had torn it up and start afresh. This was a struggle with myself.

At that time, I did not know words like 'creativity' and 'process'. And I had nothing to hand. The new generation has access to everything. They have other writers, they have periodicals. But at that time, we did not have, among the working class, any writers who could serve as an inspiration. Or those there were did not appeal to me. In any case, I was not bold enough to show them what I had written.

There was a hierarchy in which the writing coming

out of Girgaon and the writing out of Girangaon*—the mill areas—was placed. The general feeling was: what drama can there be in the mill areas, in the world of the poor? This is an area of the illiterate; how can it have space for nuance, for fluency in speech, for a tradition in culture? They are simply a labouring class. This attitude was widespread among the cultured elite, among those who had studied up to classes higher than the fourth standard. After having read almost every poem written on the working class in India, I came to the conclusion that they were based on false assumptions or were highly romanticized depictions. If the reality described in them were scrubbed a little, its base metal would show up; it would be found superficial, affected and untrue. My ambitions were vast but I had no idea whether I would be able to get the right words in the right order to achieve my aims. This was the wild struggle I was going through at the time. At least Gorky had his Kotlenko† who turned him from being a poet into a novelist. A writer must know what he is cut out to do, he must know where he belongs; otherwise he writes randomly, and if he continues to write, he might even grow in stature, but if one examines his work closely, one will find a mess of words.

---

* Girgaon is seen as traditionally being a Brahmin area; Girangaon is a working-class area, deriving its name from the mills which were situated there.

† I have transliterated this as it appeared. This may refer to Vladimir Korolenko (1853–1921), a writer, thinker and activist said to have been an important influence in Gorky's life.

In *Mother*, Gorky created the immortal revolutionary heroine, Pelagueya Vaslova. I know hundreds of activists like her. They work; they build the movement; they become martyrs. That they have never been deflected from their chosen path by unemployment or police brutality has been their great gift to the movement. It is not just working women's energy and enthusiasm that should be praised. Their magnificent lives should also be recorded. They made a huge contribution to the movement. Their hunger for cultural expression was immense. Just as Pelagueya would read everything simply so that she might know, this bunch of people had great curiosity—and it seemed it could not be satisfied simply by their cultural heritage.

In reality, it was a class that had been conscientized, but it had never been felt that they could appreciate fine literature or become responsive audiences. Their cultural development was not taken into account. It had not been thought to develop their innate talents and skills.

The needs of a changing India and a changing Maharashtra were ignored. This unforgiveable fault was inherent in the Leftist movement too. As much as it is true that men make history, it is true that history also makes men. The movement itself has a history and I write this here so that these shortcomings can be known today and that it be known that I am ashamed of them.

As a result of that, the cultural, social and educational questions of the working class did not come into focus in the Marxist movement; for it, these questions were not important. This is not the fault of the activists. In fact, they continued to work in every field but could not fully confront these questions. Let alone taking advantage of our ancient legacy of progressive literature, the writing that stretches from the saint-poets right up to the modernist movement, the changing scenarios of a changing Maharashtra were never really touched upon. The Marxists could not take into account the realist and the progressive traditions in their vision for the movement. Mahatma Jotirao Phule wrote his akhandas in order to communicate his message to the people. Dalit sections started creating jalsas—medleys of music, performance and poetry—during the time of the Satyashodhak Samaj and even under the leadership of Dr Ambedkar. It will of course be impossible to deny the role of the Communist movement in the revival of the folk theatre movement. But it is also true that all this amounted to very little. The thin trickle it engendered, always changing direction, or being made to change direction, could not be kept flowing. That it could not find *new* directions and new forms is also true. No cultural thought can survive on so little. It must flower in many ways and forms for it to become layered and only then may one claim that one has helped to change people from within and without.

You might ask why I am saying all this. My observations, the things that surrounded me, made me who I am; they have a bearing on my life. I was reading people, I was a witness, an insignificant witness, to their lives. I sat on many pavements with them and discussed things with them, and often disagreed with them, but still, I continued to live with and among them. I was one of them. I would stick posters with them. During strikes, I would picket with them. And I would plonk a bench down outside the gates of the mills and issue receipts of union dues by the flickering light of a lantern, fight elections with them, participating with enthusiasm in their rallies. This was a matter of pride for me.

The joy and unity which one feels when marching with a revolutionary group in one of its rallies, the sense it gives one of becoming stronger, so that one may achieve one's aims and objectives—this I have found to be far more inspirational than any book.

It is then that one becomes a 'we', truly a 'we', a unit. And then the world is our oyster. It is as if together we celebrate the festival of our dreams and desires.

But the Great Strike of 1942, the Naval Ratings Mutiny of 1946 and the endless excitement of Independence in 1947 were all besmirched by the communal riots that came with such events. Did the British really give us our Independence or did they trick us?

What was going to happen now, in the time that followed? Would there be a truly socialist government? Or would there be, yet again, an extortionate ruling class with a feudal mindset? Would the moneyed still rule? How were we to destroy a social order created by the caste system? How were future cultural and educational institutions to be shaped? What was going to happen in these spheres? The entire nation was discussing these issues. We were all told, political activists and others who were working in the realms of art and literature, that we would now reach the zenith of achievement. But everyone was also confused about what to do. Still, there was excitement and enthusiasm among the people.

The folk theatre movement began around the same time as the Quit India movement of 1942. Shahir Annabhau Sathe, Amar Sheikh and Gavankar* were all given an impetus by the need people felt for cultural self-expression. It is possible to discern its origins in the imperatives of the national Independence movement and the Communist movement. The folk theatre movement was so effective that all of Maharashtra was swept up in its fervour.† Cultural groups sprang up everywhere in the villages. Artistes portrayed many events of political and social significance from the Samyukta Maharashtra Movement to the Goa Liberation Struggle. People found the confidence to fight in these struggles. It is my firm opinion that the fountainhead of Dalit literature in Marathi can be found here; these revolutionary poets sowed the

---

* D.N. Gavankar, trade unionist, Communist and playwright who worked with the Indian People's Theatre Association (IPTA) and later helped form the Lal Baota Kalapathak (Red Flag Cultural Squad).

† There seems to be some contradiction here. Surve has described this as a 'thin trickle' earlier (see p. 32) but now says all of Maharashtra was swept up in its fervour. Could he mean, perhaps, on the national level? At this remove, it is difficult to say.

first seeds of self-confidence. I too was influenced by them for I was often in their company; I found myself gaining a new dimension with these interactions. When Annabhau's powadas* on Stalingrad or Spain, which he had beaten out even as he turned the spindle, were being sung, I would play the chakwa. At that time I could barely sing and I had no knowledge of these theatre groups, nor had I any idea of their significance. But just being around them meant that I developed a certain measure of self-confidence. I began to better appreciate how words worked, and '*Dongari Sheth*' ('My field on the hill') was the first song I wrote that expressed what I felt.

I had composed and recomposed songs before this, but it was only with '*Dongari Sheth*' that I succeeded in creating something that satisfied me, a song that was true to form, composed of words that lent themselves to singing but also drew their strength from the larger rural context. These were words which voiced the pains of labour but in a direct and true expression of compassion, and which, without denigrating labour, spoke of how, for all the strain, it was practically impossible to earn one's bread with it.

I discovered a way to express myself. I found a nerve I could touch. In '*Dongari Sheth*', the universal pain of women was given voice and the simple folk tune to which it was set made it easy to sing. This song reached every

* A powada is a ballad meant to be sung. It generally deals with historical events.

home. It resonated with women of every class; they would even dance to it and eventually it made its way into the commercial tamasha.

Shahir Amar Sheikh took it to every village and town. The record of it sold out immediately. At that time, in 1956, I was paid an honorarium of fifteen rupees. It seemed like a huge amount of money then. But then another great thing happened. The song was on everyone's lips, it is true, but the name of the author was forgotten. I liked that. The people took my song and made it theirs by making it into a folk song. Who remembers the writers of those old popular traditional songs? This was an honour indeed.

I had been a close observer of the ups and downs of the movement and also of the events in the cultural world. But now, as a poet myself, I began to grow. It was as if I had been given a lantern to light my path to poetry. Songs and then poems became my guiding light. I began to study Annabhau Sathe's songs and minutely examined their structure. I wanted to write songs that were as effective as his. Whether he wrote political class-based songs or nature songs, whether he turned his hand to the laavni or the powada, his work was structured and powerful. He had a wide knowledge of folk forms; and his use of colloquial speech was so eloquent that language itself would see it as an ornament.

And so I wrote many songs. '*Girnichi laavni*' ('Song of the mill') is from that period. '*Maharashtrachya naavaana*' ('In the name of Maharashtra') was to be sung as a gondhal to the tune of the saambhal.* I wrote about fifteen or twenty songs during this period and those which I thought had some spark—in other words, those that had something vital, which had a complete form and which would not evaporate with time—these I put together in my first collection, *Aisa Gaa Mee Brahma* ('Just such a Brahma am I'). But who knows why, not even one of those songs worked. When I think about it, I feel it may be because I am not a *quick* poet. I cannot write poems spontaneously. You have to have the constitution for that; or a certain attitude. I had neither. I had a store of tunes but I could not lose myself in them and 'create'. Quite naturally, then, I began to withdraw from composing and I began to think carefully about the construction and design of poetry. I steeped myself in the study of the construction of poetry, and in the process, discovered the joy of the labour of creation. It was a miracle of sorts to be able to put into words what you discovered by probing yourself, by asking reality the way forward, being true to its aches and pains, the throb and pulse of its diverse streams, being honest and at the same time tender. It is necessary to approach every moment of creation as a new person. The situation is similar to a pregnant woman's. Every new poem is like the embryo growing in her womb, bringing her both pain and joy. One sees the truth of why Keshavsut, comparing

* A gondhal is a retelling of mythological narrative stories in folk form. A sambhal is a pair of drums, one higher than the other.

a poem to the strike of a bolt of lightning, says, 'Ninety-nine per cent of those who try to catch a poem are turned to ashes.' He must have had this revelation in the moment of creation, or so I believe. But this danger is part of the capacity to create. However, several problems arise with this.

Every poem is rooted in the soil of reality. If a poem is mature, it will not prove unproductive. It will say something new. In fact, it creates new ideas, a new language, a new reality. But while this is being created, any number of complexities may present themselves, each waiting to trip the poet up. You must now protect yourself from these while preserving the spirit of the poem, for you are engaged in production and like a sculptor you must give the poem structure and life.

This is not as simple as it seems. You could call it an internal struggle. You might even go so far as calling it the struggle of creation. The poet must engage with all manner of people, their feelings and all the edges and corners of their lives; the poet must pay attention to the minute and nuanced hues of creation, he must clear the ground from which a poem may arise. When one says an artist has been corrupted or a poem does not work, what is one saying? It is not a question of whether too much was written or too little; the crux of the matter is: has it presented us with a new experience? Has it opened up a new world before us? Has it given us a new darshan of life? And even while producing this transcendent experience, many dead ends may present themselves. Words can offer us different seductions and then abandon us in the jungle. One might get sucked into the vortex of the image; sometimes in the name of novelty, one may actually begin to produce solipsistic critiques of one's own writing and one must be careful about this. Only inasmuch as poetry or literature is a product of self-criticism, only insofar as it has the sharp edge of reality can it mean something; else it becomes sound and fury signifying nothing. And sometimes one's own unwarranted opinions may be shaped into critiques. It either becomes a sham or a meaningless idealization; one begins to get bogged down in fashionable frustration or romantic revolution. Reality slips away, history slips away, human beings slip away, ideas and creation too. If one can avoid all these and go on in search of a real poem, as a humble supplicant whose feet are planted firmly on the ground and eyes screwed up to focus better on brutal, burning reality…then, somewhere, one finds oneself in front of the right door. Not only as a poet but even as an aficionado, one must find one's way to this clarity. I repeat this often to myself and whenever I find myself with a work of art in my hands, whether of my own making or of someone else's, it becomes a celebration. There's no greater or truer joy in the world than this.

I began a life in poetry. I began to forge a relationship with words. And words began to reciprocate. I have always been in the habit of reading everything that came to hand. But most of all, I enjoy reading poetry and literary debates. I read everything I could lay my hands on, on the economic, social and political issues of the day, taking in all shades of opinion. I read biographies of people whose lifestyles were opposed to my spirit. Even in these antithetical viewpoints, if I found something new, or a new approach that seemed worthy of reflection, I would offer them my careful attention. The hidden corners of people's minds appear in different forms all the time. Sometimes I would look with suspicion even upon thinking that seemed to harmonize with mine. I came across many pompous pieces too. But even in these one might find something important.

[…]

I have lived several years as an activist in the pre-Independence era and have spent some time in independent India too. I have grown up among the working class. I felt that it was my duty not just to paint pictures of the working class but also to call to account those who strip the common man of India naked, those who exploit, oppress or harass him. It was my duty to record the sorrows of the oppressed. Casteism is our biggest curse and religion has given the gods false power. We must attack the basis of human ignorance and traditional practices and the misuse of religious fervour. I bore all this in mind as I tried to put into my poems a host of new characters, new ideas and strong people. We must envisage the future constantly; I tried to do this by depicting people using their language, their lives and struggles. My 'Butcher' tells the truth that he has experienced. He says:

'Human life? That's cheap.
Mutton? That's expensive.
Life is dark, son, dark.

'To live for words, you need heart enough.
And here we are: with snouts in the trough.'

He tells the truth but he does not tell of his lot in a manner that seeks our sympathy. He is in a state of affliction but the piss and vinegar is still in him. He is one of the true witnesses of the riots that followed as a result of Independence. He loses his leg trying to save a Hindu woman and he tells the boy next door of the importance of making words come alive. In 'Money order', the woman who speaks is a victim of circumstance and lives a terrible life that she would not have chosen for herself:

Look, I feel like laughing.
Should I say all this or not?
One day, a customer came and said:
'Instead of staying here,
Come and be my wife.'
I said: 'Aren't I here for you?'
When I said that, he shuddered.
And I felt like laughing
at all the men of the world.
This terrible hide of ours
draws men like leeches;
they can say anything they like.
I feel like laughing at men
And I feel like weeping.

What she catalyses with her speech, I have witnessed myself and it has shaken me to the core. This woman who can bear this huge burden of sorrow, a mighty stone upon her chest, and yet tell the story of her life, what is she? Who is she? Is she only female, only a woman? What is her class position? There is no point in prettifying grief and trying to elicit sympathy. My people have gone beyond that. There are hundreds of these people inside my head. They tire me. I have spent many nights talking with them, arguing with them, sitting close to their lives which are hot as furnaces or even volcanoes; all this only to listen to their profound stories. They are my holy books, my scriptures, my gurus. This is an endless piece of luck that has fallen to my lot. It makes me happy.

First we must learn to love our fellow man. This must be a real feeling. Then people will open up to you. They will take your words and nurse them in their hearts, they will repeat them. The hands of the workers may be soiled but their interior landscapes are not. I have been witness to many instances when writers have alienated workers and this grieves me. And then I become pensive. What I write here are my own experiences as I have understood them. It is not to exalt myself. Nothing is to be gained from self-promotion or from aggression. You must prove what you say. And to prove it, you must respect the most important rule, which is the love of one's fellow man.

Our discussions, heated, intense though they may be, must continue. We must fight the battles of art and ideology, tooth and nail. This had not been happening, but now, fortunately, it has begun. Creation must contend with creation. Complete acceptance is as fruitless a space as complete rejection. It is essential for us to be in a state of total awareness to live and to write. And it is important for us to talk about our beautiful liberal legacy, which has been preserved for us by various progressive movements. The Independence movement, the revolutions initiated by Mahatma Jotirao Phule and Dr Ambedkar, the Communist and the Socialist movements have carved out an important history for us. In the field of literature, important spaces have been opened up by a variety of voices which may be found in the writings of the poet-saints right up to Keshavsut and the modernism of Haribhau Apte.*

It is of them that we must ask the way forward. We must reject the debased. We must adapt ourselves to the new and changing reality. How heavy a responsibility history has placed upon us and how bright the coming era is, we will only learn in the future.

I do not say all this in self-defence. It is not as if I hold a brief for my poems either. That is not necessary. If a creation is taken into a living heart and it settles there, it will remain alive in the hearts of the people and in history. This much is certain. Attempts to blow one's own trumpet often seem like trying to make music with a carrot. So the question of saving such art does not arise. Real art is

* Hari Narayan Apte (1864–1919) was a novelist and short story writer.

self-generated and self-sustaining. Nor is it my contention that what I have created is 'immortal literature'. What I have constructed has come out of three considerations: myself, poetry and reality as I saw and experienced it. So you might call this a reinvestigation of my life within a life, or the clumsy journey of my life with its many false steps and dead ends. There has been no false humility on display here. Nor has there been any aggressive moral posturing. What I saw, I wrote.

I have always watched out for any signs of arrogance. For life is much harder than even my understanding of it. It is more hideous and more difficult and it will take new artists and their new creations to bring that to light. I only hope that I will be able to confront the new revolutionary age with my head held high. The reality I have faced and my poetry has surely given me that much courage.

NARAYAN SURVE

‘Ghalib is Ghalib, but my Islya is also Islya’

Narayan Surve interviewed by Shanta Gokhale and Devendra Balsaraf

This interview was conducted around 2002 by Shanta Gokhale as preparation for the making of the film Narayan Gangaram Surve, *a project that she initiated—she also wrote the script—though it was directed by Arun Khopkar. I have edited it very lightly because what comes across is two friends talking to each other, and when I read an interview which has that quality of spontaneous conversation, I have the delightful feeling that I am a licensed eavesdropper. There are times one might have liked to check back with Surve, to ask what he meant, but since the poet is no longer with us, we must make do with such riches as are available and say in one's head: stet.*

(Also present was Devendra Balsaraf, assistant to Arun Khopkar.)

Excerpts from the interview

Shanta Gokhale: You mention living in a place called Bogdyanchi Chawl [the Chawl of Tunnels]…

Narayan Surve: It's still there, behind the cancer hospital. Actually, it belonged to a Parsi, but he died without heirs and the municipal corporation took it over. They appointed a supervisor who would collect rents. Now, why Bogdyanchi Chawl? Because it was really like a tunnel. If you went in…here a tunnel, there a tunnel, everywhere tunnel after tunnel. That's how things get named: the man on the street names things to reflect his observations. For instance, a mill was called Kelyachi Girni because of the banana trees that grew there. The mills did not spring up today; they have been there for a hundred years. So the old workers use the language they coined as youngsters. Now, Sahar Road was called Coal Dongri [Coal Hill] because there was a huge pile of coal on it; you won't see it now. But people distort the originals and invent their own names.

SG: How long did you live there?

NS: Krishnabai and I fell in love and got married. That means we had to fight society and go to court to get married. At that time, I was an activist in the [trade union] movement. So the question [that was put to my wife] was, 'He's got no one, no relatives, no family, no prospects. Where do you think you're going?' Society, fifty years ago, was a lot harder about these things. I could not even state my caste. I did not know who my father was. I could not say what religion I had been born into. I had no home, no native place, no origins, for I had been abandoned on the streets. The mill workers who took me in gave me my name, my caste, gave me my age. That was my history, see? Even so, I had become part of the trade union movement, and as an activist, I would hold meetings. [One of Krishnabai's uncles] was in the Communist movement and so we went to stay with him after we got married.

I'm not about to tell you how we fell in love and how we eloped. It was a difficult time. Today, questions of caste are still difficult but some of the walls are coming down. Now, love marriages can be seen all over the place. There is still social opposition but it is much more subdued. But at that time we had to face opposition from the local people. My adoptive father, Gangaram Surve, called all the village folk and gave them tea in aluminium tamrels.* That was when we took a room in Chandivalya Chawl. I was a peon in a municipal school at the time.

SG: How did you get the job?

NS: At first, I was a peon in the [education] department but then I went to Bori Bunder. After 1950, the typing department was shifted there. Before that the city stretched up to Bandra. Now, it became Greater Bombay and Greater Bombay went up to Borivali, and it went on growing, taking in Dahisar and then Bhayander. At that time, the education officer was Kapilabai Khandvala,† a leftist. She would help all the activists of the movement.

* It is likely that this was an act of appeasement for his adoptive son's disruptive behaviour. A tamrel is a mug.

† Kapila Khandvala was 'a great educationist who was the first lady inspector for schools in the 60s and she was known for her strong views on women empowerment and discrimination'. You can read more about her work on the official website of the college named after her, Smt Kapila Khandvala College of Education (www.kkcoe.edu.in).

Mirajkar[*] was the mayor of Bombay and the movement was roaring along… In 1944, when a ship exploded, we went to help, truck after truck of us, and we spent the night there.[†] That was 1944, fifty-eight years ago. So my age [now] must be anything between 72 and 75.

Because I could not tell them anything about my caste or my age, some people would get very angry with me. At the same time, some people were sympathetic. Society was very conservative and so was the Communist Party. I stayed with the Party nevertheless, fighting and struggling along, though there were terrible times…

The Communist Party expelled me. [It was as if they were saying,] 'If a Communist activist were to marry such a woman, what would be the effect on the masses?' That was their theory.

SG: But were there any real reasons?

NS: Not that I could tell. The Party ordered me to leave her. I said I would not. I told them I had married her.

---

* This refers to Shantaram Savlaram Mirajkar, among the earliest leaders of the Communist Party of India. He became the mayor of Bombay in 1958.

† The *SS Fort Stikine*, a ship laden with gunpowder, cotton and gold bars, sailed into Bombay's harbour and exploded after the cotton caught fire in April 1944. Many citizens thought the city was being bombed. See also Daya Pawar's account of the moment in *Baluta* (Speaking Tiger, 2016) and Vandana Mishra's account in *I, the Salt Doll* (Speaking Tiger, 2016). Surve's comment points to the initiative and energy of the activists associated with the Left movement at the time.

Now, I was lying, but it was a white lie. And so I got an employed wife; she scolds quite a lot but she is a good wife. I am what I am because of her. You never know how your life experiences are going to shape you.

SG: So where did you live [after marriage]?

NS: At the Chandivalya Chawl. Sixty to seventy years ago, you could easily get a room for seven or eight rupees. This accommodation problem has only arisen in the last forty years. After the Second World War ended, people from the Deccan Plateau began to flow into Mumbai. Before that it was only the coastal people because there was nothing in the Konkan. In comparison, the farms in the Deccan were in good shape. But that changed and the numbers began to rise.

Since I had fallen in love… A friend of mine, Shankar Jadhav, did much to help me. He lived at Santa Cruz. Later, the poor fellow went mad and died. He was a peon in a municipal school…

I believe in gratitude. You will find it in all my poems. Because all these people helped shape Narayan Surve. No one person does this alone. When we came to live [at the Chandivalya Chawl] it was all slum. Bhaiyas* lived here; it was a Bhaiya area. People would say that they had come to the city with a handful of channa and a lota for water. They are now millionaires. But what of it? Those who

* This is a term that is used in Mumbai for North Indians.

used their brains and made money and used it wisely and got their rewards…

From [Chandivalya] we came to Shankar's place. Shankar and I together went to Kalina where we got slum dwellings. The Mumbai University stands on that land now. There was a man there at the time called Baburao who owned a bullock-cart and had a Muslim driver. We would help him yoke his bullocks up. Krishnabai would clean the house and wash the vessels. Remember, I was a municipal peon on a salary of sixty-five rupees.

After that we had a son, we became parents, all of that… [A]ll the slums [at Kalina] were demolished—a storm ruined them—and we left and went [back] to Santa Cruz. [We moved to] Bibibai's Chawl at Khar, where a college stands now. Bibibai was a Muslim woman who would build the huts and sell them to people. It was an illegal hut built near a tank. My elder son was born there. He graduated and lives in Nashik now. But then those slums were torn down too and we lived by a pond near the chawl. There were morchas to go on and we were living on a bed beside a pond! My wife did not have a job, the child was small, the morchas were on… From there we came to live behind the station at Santa Cruz. There were no toilets so we had to go to the station to use the toilets. My elder son is fifty-one today so all this is a long time ago. Anyway, I was in the movement and I was a loquacious sort.

Kapilabai said to me, 'Narayan, you talk so well. How far have you studied?'

'Fourth standard,' I said.

'Why don't you do your finals?' she asked.

[To his wife:] Krishnabai, do you remember the morchas?

SG: Was she marching with you?

NS: Of course. We were inveterate marchers. Without a flag set on a pole, the lower classes will never survive. Sometimes the flag is the Shiv Sena's; sometimes it is the red flag,* and sometimes that of the Jana Sangh. But the flag is important; it gives you a sense of belonging. It offers you a political support structure as well.

Krishnabai, do you remember, I wrote a story on Bibibai's chawl later?

Krishnabai: He was about twenty-two years old at the time…

NS: And we had Ravindra, right?

Krishnabai: We had nothing for him, no cradle, nothing…

NS: She would hold him in her lap and I would go and work and then go on a morcha. But then we were part of the movement and this was nothing special, nothing

* He uses the term 'lal baota' for red flag; this is how most people in Maharashtra talk about Communists of every stripe.

terrible. And since we lived like that, we took it in the same spirit.

[...] Then Jeroobai Patwardhan* came along.

Khandvalabai said [one day to Jeroobai], 'What to do with this boy? He's a good speaker.'

I would make party speeches; my poems had been published.

'That's good, Narayana. Why don't you do your seventh standard examinations?' [Jeroobai asked.]

'I don't have a place to stay,' I said.

'We'll have to do something about that,' she said.

And we came to Bogdyanchi Chawl, as a special case. She is no more; she used to live at Khar. Mrs Khandvala is also no longer with us. She was a very sincere lady. She helped many people in the movement.

So there we were in Bogdyanchi Chawl... If you ever go there, you will have to wait fifteen minutes to see anything; it takes that long for your eyes to get accustomed to the darkness. The rent was eight rupees and I went back to school.

SG: The chawl was for municipal workers?

NS: No, no. Bai was in the municipality† and she used her influence. But it was about 150 square feet, no kitchen or

---

* Not much can be found on Jeroo Patwardhan. She seems to have been active in Communist circles and Parsi by birth. The editors would be grateful for any information anyone can supply about her.

† Surve uses the word 'municipality' interchangeably with 'corporation' to refer to Mumbai's municipal corporation.

anything. One room, pitch black. When Dilip Chitre shot a film on me, he filmed it there. The [Sahitya] Akademi did not give me a copy.

Now there are so many awards and honours. I have no idea what to do with them. There's Dnyaneshwar, Ganpati Bappa, Gautam Buddha, Lenin and Dr Ambedkar inside. One day a friend said, 'You have all the gods and revolutionaries in your home.'

I said: 'That's what our country is.'

But it is a difficult question: what to do with all of them?

Devendra Balsaraf: Your office was also there?

NS: The Party office was in the Dalvi Building, near the BDD [Bombay Development Department] Chawls. Ambedkar used to live there at some point. He studied there under the staircase, by the light of streetlamps. That's part of history. There is still a market there but it must all have been renovated now.

SG: So how many years did you stay at Bogdyanchi Chawl?

NS: Ten to fifteen years. After that I became a teacher…

SG: So you did your final exams?

NS: I joined night school and sat for my seventh standard exams. This was the Utkarsh Night High School in Byculla.

There was a teacher there by the name of Narkar; he's dead too. He would encourage me, saying: 'You speak well.' It was a progressive night high school, right near the Byculla Station. Look how many years have passed. I was a teacher for nineteen years and it has been twenty-two years since I retired... Narkar kept saying I should study. But honestly, I too used to feel: how long can I remain a peon in a school? She [indicating Krishnabai] also insisted. She called me 'Master' already. This was because I would conduct meetings and whoever spoke at the meeting was the 'master'. And among the workers, I was the one who had studied up to the fourth standard and that was quite a lot of education!

I had worked there fourteen years already. That was not very good. I had just begun writing poetry and people were beginning to praise my work. They were beginning to ask, 'Who has written these poems? We should find out.'

So I joined night school and came to the Municipal School Library and got my primary school teachers' certificate...they teach the DEd* course there. [V.P.] Kulkarni was the principal. It was a two-year course. At that time, they would accept students who had passed the seventh standard. You could finish your seventh standard, do your primary teacher training, go to the village and get yourself a small government job. Today, engineers find themselves unemployed!

---

* Diploma in Education, a certificate course that can be pursued after the plus-two examinations or the twelfth standard, which trains teachers for elementary school.

I was twenty-nine years when I passed the DEd. I had two sons and Krishnabai on my ration card at the time. I sat for the seventh standard at the same time as my son did. The elder son was at the Vernacular Final SSC stage. Now, one of my grandsons is in the eleventh, my grand-daughters are both graduates. Their grandfather only studied up to the fourth standard!

Now that I am famous, when I go to the school in which I was a peon, people say, 'Look, Master has come! Master has come!'

I went to the Gurdwara High School to sit for my exams. All around me were these little boys and I was twenty-nine.* In those days the SSC students would be asked to invigilate at these exams. They were very suspicious of me. 'Who is this mature man who has come to sit for the exams?' they must have been thinking.

The girl [invigilating] asked me, 'Who do you want to speak to?'

I said, 'I want to sit for the examination.'

She wrote a note and sent me off to the supervisor. This was in 1957 or '58. When the head supervisor came, he brought along a policeman. At that time, the Vernacular Final Exam would have at least one policeman around. Now it's become even more strict. Back then,

---

* Surve says that he was twenty-nine at this point and earlier that he was twenty-nine when he sat for his seventh standard examinations. It is possible that the chronology might not have been clear in his head or that he sat for both examinations in the same year, one after the other, to get his qualification as a teacher.

policemen looked strange; they wore those short pants with a baton in their belt; their headgear was a royal pugree.

'What do you want?' he asked.

'To sit for the exam. I am a night school student. Look, I have my hall-ticket with me.'

'What were you doing all these years?'

I lost my temper. 'Screwing around,' I said.

He realized there was no point arguing with me and that I had all my papers with me so I got to sit for the exam.

The next day the boys were saying to each other, 'What a big fat man has come!'

So at the Raja Shivaji High School annual awards function, I said, 'The Narayan Surve you suspected [of cheating] is now the guest of honour here.'

When I was expelled from the movement, it caused some comment: '*Arre*, he's such an intelligent man and you're expelling him.' And so I decided I would push back and see what happened. This became a habit with me: to stand my ground and see what happens.

When I was presented with the Kabir Samman by Digvijay Singh,* I said: 'I don't know whether Kabir ever went to school but my father had me educated up to the fourth standard. Kabir's adoptive father was also a weaver. The man who picked me off a rubbish heap was a mill

* Congress member of parliament who was chief minister of Madhya Pradesh from 1993 to 2003. Surve won the Kabir Samman—an award established by the Madhya Pradesh government in 1986–87 to 'honour poetic genius in the field of Indian poetry'—in 1999.

worker. At base, a mill worker and a weaver are the same. Six hundred years have passed since the adoption of Kabir and now you give me this award. Are you sure you're in your right minds?' *Hindustan Times* splashed the news on their pages. Today, I am on the committee that gives the award.

As a teacher, I got the opportunity to study children at first hand, their conversation, their ways of speaking, their behaviour.

On the fourth day [of the exam] I nearly missed the boat. At that time, drawing was a compulsory subject. (Now my grandson can draw fine pictures.) I suppose it was compulsory because it would come in handy wherever you were. I just sat there because I could not even draw a straight line. But by now the young girl had come to the conclusion that I was a decent human being and not a fraud.

So she said, 'What are you sitting around for?'

'I can't draw at all,' I said.

'What do you mean you can't draw?' she said. 'You'll fail if you don't draw. You must draw.'

And she guided me through it—a sari border pattern, a still life and a memory drawing. And I passed—59.5 per cent, a decent showing. What I regret is that I never asked that girl's name. I realize now that it was because of her that I passed that exam and got a government job and became a school master.

So then I was a Master, and then they called me Guruji and now Sir. These are differences in language…

Later, I got to the BEd level. [I had come a long way from when] Khandvalabai said: 'Pass the seventh standard and then let's see.' Perhaps she thought I was an intelligent man. I have found that if you are willing to do what is right, people will come forward to help you. People are not without their good sides; or else the world would collapse. So I filled in the form...the principal was V.P. Kulkarni who lived at Shivaji Park, Dadar. He was a follower of [Acharya] Atre* and part of the Samyukta Maharashtra movement. And being in the movement, my stories and poems were being printed. So he gave me permission [to work and study at the same time].

I had said I would leave the job for two years and study for my BEd. I would not work anywhere else for the period I was studying. Here I was, a peon at a municipal school. It seemed impossible. Krishnabai had just started on a job Khandvalabai had found her.

Back then, we had to learn how to use the charkha, or spinning wheel. The boys in the training college called it Sootakbai;† it was a paper. The spinning teacher was Rane and Nimbalkar Sir taught us stitching. [I was never in class] so he reported this to Mr Kulkarni who knew me distantly from the movement. He called me and said, 'Someone has reported that you are never present for that class. Tell me honestly what the problem is.'

---

* Prahlad Keshav Atre (1898–1969) was a noted writer, poet, editor and founder of the paper, *Maratha.* He was part of the Samyukta Maharashtra Movement as well.

† 'Mrs Spinning', she must have been a hard teacher to please.

Once again, I discovered the humanity inherent in mankind.

'Tell me the truth, Surve. I know you from your poem, *Dongari Sheth*,' he said.

I had written that poem in 1956. In 1959, I sat for my primary teachers' certificate exam, and so, he must have heard my name.

'To tell the truth, sir, I am a peon in a municipal school.'

'Haven't you left your job? That's the rule.'

'I am a poor man, sir. I don't know how else to do this.'

V.P. Kulkarni is no longer with us but he looked after me. He told Nimbalkar and Rane: 'You will not mark him; I will give him his marks.' And there too I passed with 57.5 per cent. And actually, my spinning was done at home by Bai here. I would take her work and present it as my own. I needed something to show. Sometimes, we even bought some at Khadi Bhandar! I did all this because I wanted to study. This is how you have to make your life.

When there was an inspection, I said I would teach something outside the syllabus. The inspector was also an external examiner, but part of the government. I chose to teach my poem '*Aai*' ['Mother']— someone had written on it in *Sakaal*. The children were working class, the community outside was working class and so was the mother in the poem. But the students said nothing. They were silent, they gave no answers. And your score depended on how much they answered. But the inspector was moved. He said, 'You need not say any more,' and he gave me very good marks. He had tears in his eyes. I have no idea whether it is a good poem or not but many people have told me that it appeals to them; it touches their hearts.

In 1961, with Khandvalabai's help, I went from being a peon to being a teacher at the Naigaon School Number 1. For four days after I joined they did not assign me a class. What could a peon-turned-teacher teach? Finally, they gave me a class full of failures. But to my good luck, *Aisa Gaa Mee Brahma* won a State award and everyone decided I was okay. Political people [*sic*] have made these rules.

SG: So your colleagues felt differently about you once you received the State award?

NS: It came to their attention that I was now a teacher. Different perhaps, but still a teacher.

SG: Were your colleagues involved in the decision to give you or not give you a class?

NS: The principal of the school had to make that decision, right? If the principal looks down on a peon; he will treat you in a certain way. If he has a different way of looking…

So he gave me the students who were failing—that

was his attitude. This does not change. It is there in all classes. It's not as if only Brahmins have it; Dalits have it too. It's the outcome of the early socialization of a person. If a person does not develop a liberal, thoughtful outlook, then they stay the same. Perhaps he had had a bad experience earlier so he treated me as a lesser human being. He harassed me, but I was determined too.

I had a meeting with under-graduate students from Chicago; Abhay Sardesai* organized it. The students were here to study the various cities: Mumbai, Calcutta, Delhi. Some were European, others were of Indian origin but were residents of America. I said, 'I don't speak any English,' but they said I was not to worry. The main teacher was very encouraging. We talked for about an hour and a half through translators. They met me and some others...and then left for Kolkata. They had read some translations of my work in *World Literature Today*. Someone from Osmania University had translated my poems. Five or six of my poems have been translated into French. When the magazine editor came to the Elphinstone College, he said he wanted to meet Narayan Surve. So I read some of my poems to him.

... I was still a fourth-standard pass when N.R. Phatak† once said to me, 'You write well, re.' 'My field on the

---

* Abhay Sardesai is a Mumbai-based poet, translator and editor of the magazine, *Art India*.

† Narahar Raghunath Phatak (1893–1979) was best known for his biographies, of Mahadeo Govind Ranade, Bal Gangadhar Tilak and Yashwantrao Holkar, among others.

hill' had become very popular at the time. Phatak was a progressive historian and a good person. He and Potdar* were a team. Phatak's tongue was a weapon. He said I should study further so I went to the Sahitya Sangh office; there is a theatre there now.

Whoever the secretary was, he asked me, 'What do you want?'

I said I wanted [to study] to become a teacher.

'How far have you studied?' he said.

'Fourth standard,' I said, and even as I said it, I thought, 'I'm trespassing here. I'm an interloper.'

'Fourth standard? What grammar can you know?' he asked.

I was clean-bowled.

'If you don't know grammar, how will you pass these exams?' he asked. 'We can't admit you.'

So I went back to meet Kaka and N.R. Phatak who were truly enraged. He called him and gave him a thorough dressing down. Kaka was a real gentleman. He gave the man a lecture on the great people of Mumbai and mentioned me as one of them.

'He is a chaprasi in a municipal school but he writes good stories and good songs.'

He gave me the money for the examination. Where was I going to find the fees [otherwise]? He got me the books. He called the Sangh up and said, 'Surve is coming,

---

* Dattatray Vaman Potdar (1890–1979) was a historian and writer. He served as the Vice-Chancellor of Pune University and was awarded the Padmabhushan.

let him in.' I went seven days later. If I hadn't gone, I would have had it from him. I did confess, finally, that I was not going to sit for the examinations. I just wanted to know what this grammar was that I did not know.

I do not see myself as knowledgeable. I am uneducated. But I will not accept that the person in front of me is knowledgeable simply because he has a degree.

Now, it was my turn for a rare dressing down from Kaka.

Some years after I won the State award, I was chief guest at a ceremony in which awards were conferred upon students. I could not have appeared in it in my grammar-free state! In 1966, 'My university' came out and won four awards including the Nehru Award, the Soviet Land Award, the Mehta Award, etc. Now I have won 22 awards. Sometimes I look back and think…in 1967, the Akhil Bharatiya Sahitya Mahamandal put my book on the syllabus, the book of a man with no grammar!

And one last joke: in 1995, the writers made me president of the Akhil Bharatiya Sahitya [Sammelan]!

SG: Before you started writing, were you reading?

NS: I was reading, of course. I was reading reference books in the library about the Communist movement. S.V. Deshpande* was our teacher. We listened to his lectures.

---

* Shankar Vaman Deshpande was a freedom fighter and a member of the Communist Party.

In the 1942 Quit India Movement, in the People's Volunteer Brigade, Ishwarbhai Patel was our leader. He was a Congresswallah. We were all equals. Batlivala* gave me a pair of trousers which were loose. He was in the Congress too and came to the trade union movement. All these people were with the Congress in those days and slowly came to the Communist movement... I tied up those trousers with a piece of rope and went to August Kranti Maidan to see how Gandhi looked. There was a lathi charge there. When the first lathi fell on my back, I realized how bad the British government was... [So that] was when I saw Gandhi.

What did Gandhi look like? What did Nehru look like? This is how I educated myself. It is a habit I have not lost. This is what my poetry is like.

And so, going on in this fashion, I would attend classes. Afterwards, I joined Kohinoor Mill No 3 near Shiv Sena Bhavan as a 'doffer boy'. There was a special night school for working kids which I joined. I must have been about twelve or thirteen.

SG: In your poem, 'Mumbai', you say you took your father's place at the same machine when he died.

NS: [T]hey did not hire me in his place. I started as a worker, like everyone else. My adoptive parents were

* This may refer to Soli Batlivala, member of the Communist Party of India. For more details of his life in culture, see Shanta Gokhale, *The Scenes We Made: An Oral History of Experimental Theatre in Mumbai* (Speaking Tiger, 2015).

mill workers. They brought me up until I was eleven or twelve… When I was eleven or twelve, [my mother, Kashibai] put ten rupees into my hands and said, 'Take this and fill your stomach.' They went off to the village but they did come back. When they died, they were with me. Krishnabai got them admitted to a hospital. I was a member of the State Textbook Committee at the time and was in Pune for a meeting. They were very proud that I was successful.

When I won the Kabir Samman and was awarded the Padma Shri, the reporter from Delhi's *Hindustan Times* asked me what the most beautiful moment in my life was. I said it was lighting my father's funeral pyre—as if I were truly his own son, a rite which is held to be the holiest there is. My parents had one biological child; Sakhu teaches in Damodar Hall School.

SG: You were ten or twelve years old when they left. Where did you live?

NS: Under the staircase at night, and during the day, wherever I could. Later, there were relatives. Vaman Sawant, who wrote stories, was with the Young Friends' League in Mahim and I got work there. I swept the floors and did things like that.

SG: And then you moved to a mosque…

NS: Yes, that was the time. This was my first introduction to Muslim people. As boys, we would go to Mahim, to the small beach behind the dargah where there would also be an urs.

We went to bathe in the sea [once] and left our clothes underneath the rocks. When we came back, a fakir had stolen our clothes. There I was, naked as the day I was born. So I went and hid amid the graves in the Muslim cemetery… At the time of prayer they must cover their heads. When I went to the gurudwara in Nanded, we had to remove the cigarettes from our pockets, and if our heads were uncovered, we had to put cloth on our heads… Out of the four or five [people at the cemetery], one of them heard me scuffling about behind the gravestones. He got up and roared, 'Who's there?'

I emerged with my hands folded.

'You're naked? Don't you have any shame?'

I said, 'A fakir stole…'

'*Achcha, achcha.* Come here.'

He gave me a towel, one of those they use when they pray. I used that towel in my poem 'Usman Bhai' [*sic*], about how they carry a towel on which they kneel to pray.

'Idiot. Don't ever come into a mosque naked again,' he said, 'Or I'll beat you.'

But he let me go away with the towel wrapped around me. That's when I realized Muslims are not bad people.

SG: What does a doffer boy do?

NS: In the winding department there are 41,500 spindles that are constantly turning. If one stops, the machine stops. The doffer boy's job was to run up and unstuck the spindle, pull off whatever yarn has stuck and let the spindles turn again. Then they reconnect the thread. Sometimes the ends of the thread have to be removed. That was the doffer boy's job; he was on the lowest rung of the pecking order. The job left calluses on my hands. So I used the image of the callus in my poem. There are calluses on the hands of the carpenter, on the hands of the ironsmith, but there are none on the hands of the supervisor. It is the difference in the work they do.

SG: By this time, you had finished your fourth standard.

NS: I finished the fourth standard in 1936. In 1961, I became a teacher. All my age-related details are approximations. [Gangaram] Surve would say, 'This is my adopted son.' Whenever I wrote a book, I would say that I had been adopted.

[Pointing to his wife:] They would tease her and say, 'Look at our Narayan and you!'

Krishnabai: I had four uncles, he had no one at all. There was no chance of my getting out of the house.

NS: She would take the ration card and go out, as if to check whether the rations had come. And then we would wander about together.

Krishnabai: He had no money at all and I was in the same situation. I would wash vessels and do jobs like that. And Ajji [her grandmother] was also at home. Back then, girls were not supposed to go out of the house after six-thirty pm. Nor were they educated. They would say: If we send you to school, where will we find a husband for you?

NS: Where would one find an educated husband? That was the social situation…

Krishnabai: I came from a good family but all my uncles were drunkards. And it was the uncles who would fix the marriages. But although I was illiterate as a child, I was rather clever. I decided that it would be better for me if I chose someone for myself rather than accepting someone they chose for me.

NS: [To Krishnabai:] Good you did that…

I learned that there was a municipal settlement for workers here and the municipality would give you an eighty per cent loan at six per cent interest. So I did my best and came to Santa Cruz. As this was on an ownership basis, it remains in your name.

I won the Nehru Award twice, once for '*Mazhe Vidyapeeth*' ['My university'] and once for '*Jahirnama*' ['Manifesto']. In 1976, I paid ten thousand rupees and settled down here; and I caught the aeroplane from here as well.

SG: Did you not get transferred from the school?

NS: No, the Corporation left me alone. I only worked at two schools: one was Naigaon Number 1 and [the other was] at Jagganath Bhatankar Marg near Damodar Hall. Mrs Kamath was the Education Officer at the time. Then Madhuri Shah came along.

... [This] is how I got the job of a sepoy.* The mayor was Mirajkar;† he gave me a letter and respecting the wishes of the mayor, the Corporation gave me the job. Dr Hamid was the medical officer, the municipal medical examiner [who came to examine me]. There is a chowk at Bombay Central which is named after him.

He asked me, 'Certificate?'

I said I did not have it with me at that time.

'What kind of people are you?' he said. 'Now what am I going to write as your age? Okay, go and stand near that wall.'

He measured me and then announced my age. He put me down as 1922 born. I told him my adoptive father had put me down as 1926 born.

'Now it doesn't matter,' he said.

I thought: Whatever it takes! A sepoy's job is a sepoy's job. Better than wandering about here and there. And it's a permanent job. I could get in and stick to it.

The Corporation did not trouble me much but the police did. If there was a strike in the city, the police would

---

* A sepoy in Mumbai at the time was a peon.

† There seems to be a problem with timelines here. Surve had been working as a peon long before Mirajkar became mayor in 1958. The latter may have helped out in some other capacity. But we have chosen to leave the text as it is.

be at my door first thing in the morning. And of course I would trick them. On the day there was a strike, I would definitely go to work. And as soon as work was over in the afternoon, I would get up and leave with my flag.

[Later, I became] a member of three or four universities. I was also on the Bal Bharati Board of the municipality for seven years. Then one day I got a letter telling me that I was supposed to retire because of the date, 1922, which Dr Hamid had fixed as my year of birth.

I said to Krishna, 'What do we do?'

She said, 'You just take your bag and go to school, right? Why not just retire?'

Because I was involved in so many programmes she did not believe that I was teaching at all.

Mrs Kamath* said, 'You're not at retirement age yet. Go and see the doctor. I'll give you a letter. We're losing a famous poet and this does not feel right.'

'Let it go,' I said.

I did not fight it. What would I gain? At the most, an increase in pay. Instead, I thought, now I will be able to do a little more, a few more programmes.

SG: I wanted to ask about your language… It's extremely clear and lucid.

---

* There's a chronology problem here: Mrs Kamath could not possibly have been still working when Surve was ready to retire. Perhaps she had some voluntary post-retirement position or was a board member and so was confronted with the idea of losing an award-winning member of the staff.

NS: I was reading and then thinking about language. I read all kinds and types of writers and then I chose a style for myself. If you think about it, you can acquire a style of your own. Many people have asked me: how do you achieve this simplicity in your poetry? The poems seem simple on the surface but they are also profound. In the primary school class that I taught for nineteen years, there were Malis, Kolis and the children of police constables. They had no one to instruct them on matters of high culture. If one had to teach these children, one had to use a language that was clear, clean and simple; speaking that way entered into my writing, I think.

We need to know who we are writing for; I am not writing for the scholar. What I think is inspired by how people live. There are millions of people who live like that. I should write in their kind of language.

I used a great deal of colloquial language too. There are lines from Ghalib that I have reworked for one of my characters. I remember Sahir Ludhianvi hugging me. My style of reading poetry seemed different to people; all my experiences taught me something. Ludhianvi said to me: 'What, Surve, you've turned Ghalib upside down!' Ghalib is Ghalib, but my Islya is also Islya. There are also dialects from all over Maharashtra that I have used; if I can capture the suffering of that soul then I have achieved a poem.

'*Jahirnama*' won an award in 1975 and 1976 and '*Mazhe Vidyapeeth*' in 1968... [T]here was a rule [back then]. If you were a municipality employee, any prize you won had to be deposited in the department and then it would be paid to you. I have never done that. I told them: 'Do what you want.' I had something of a reputation by that time. I was working on the principle that all I had to do was utter the name 'Narayan, Narayan'* and do what I had to. In that sense, I was entering into dialogue with myself.

In 1976, Kaifi Azmi and I were on the same flight. Kaifi was a freelancer; I had a job. It was not easy for me to take that flight... I had just learned that if a dog bit you, you could get a whole month's leave. If you developed whooping cough, you would get leave automatically. Since I had won the Nehru Award, an international award, I wrote to the Corporation asking for two weeks' leave. The Corporation's accounts department wanted proof that I had won the award even though it was all over the press. They made a huge song and dance about it: show us this; bring that and then we will think about it. Some friends intervened and leave was granted.

Later, I became president of the Akhil Bharatiya Sahitya Sammelan. I received the Nehru Award from the hands of the Vice-President. And the Padma Shri from the hands of President K.R. Narayanan. The headline then was: 'Good work! One Narayan honours another'.

---

* When he says, 'Narayan, Narayan', he is invoking the God but there are many layers to this invocation. One might say it as a blessing, one might say it as a greeting, one might say it as a talisman against trouble that seems to be brewing.

The Poems

By way of introduction

I'm run ragged, in and out.
My daily bread is my daily doubt.
I am a worker, a flashing sword,
Set to slash through the literary horde.
Don't you quiver, don't go 'Tut tut',
My sins will be venial, Mr Saraswat.

I've watched, I've heard, assessed it all.
I turned it into what you'd call
my signature scrawl.
All those learnings, losses, all that mess,
As I live, I write, so I confess.

Bread is dear but I need more.
I burn my brand into your door.
To my words, I offer flowers.
I give them swords, release their powers.

I'm not alone; our time has come.
Beware, what follows is the storm.
I am a worker, a flashing sword,
Set to slash through the literary horde.
Don't you quiver, don't go 'Tut tut',
My sins will be venial, Mr Saraswat.

I don't want your sad nights now

I don't want your sad nights now.
I rose from one such mehfil not long ago.
I was sad as I rose: but one must be sad.
The moon had set: as the moon must.

Or let me say: I turned forlorn footsteps homewards.
Or let me say: the moon waned in woe.

The flags of day began to fly.
Or let me say: they fell, enfolding us.
Or let me say: they cantered over the city, over home.

Jivba was on his bench at the gate,
lantern still alight,
counting subscriptions.*

'Hey Jivba, what long nights you keep.'
'Yeah, yeah. Eaters of fire, shitters of scorpions, that's us.
Don't give us these ghazals.'

I don't want your sad nights now.
Really, I don't.

---

* Party subscriptions.

By such treacherous light

Easy enough to adorn a life with lies you've wrought.
Such invitations came my way; not that they did not.

The seasons whistled past my door; some wet, some cold, some hot.
My words did sometimes raise their eyes; not that they did not.

Pundits hid symbols from us; the cymbals were our lot.
Many said, 'Play along, monkey song.' Not that they did not.

At each corner, another shop where honour could be bought.
There, men of fortune pawned their brains; not that they did not.

By the treacherous light the flickering flame a single candle wrought,
I walked, I walked to save myself; not that I did not.

Money order

Now look here, write like this,
Say: I'm happy; my body aches, yes;
But also say: this is better than the village.

Men gather like the clouds
and burst all over us.
But Babdi, she goes for them with:
'How many have you slept with
Before me?'
I tell her: 'He's a client, girl.
They say "sit", you sit.
Are their wives going to give them up?'

Now write:
The money order may be late
But it will come.
The vajratika has been sent to Vishnu
and fifty rupees, less ten.
From that, buy books for Gangi
And chuddies for Namya.
Give them ten paise every day
So they'll run to school.
And kiss them both for me.

Things are getting expensive here.
Each john wants a fresh sheet.
Not enough now to freshen up
The bed with some water
And offer a soft shoulder.
They want fans now.
Don't write that.
You're listening, that's why I'm talking.
Look, I feel like laughing.
Should I say all this or not?
One day, a customer came and said:
'Instead of staying here,
Come and be my wife.'
I said: 'Aren't I here for you?'
When I said that, he shuddered.
And I felt like laughing
at all the men of the world.
This terrible hide of ours
draws men like leeches;
they can say anything they like.
I feel like laughing at men
And I feel like weeping.
They crave this hide.
They're like animals,
They can't help it.

You must be bored, listening to me.
Everything here is boring.
Come when you can.
Come up and see me some time.

Poster

The night is a dodderer on its last legs
When four of us leave
From four homes.

'Hanmya, take this ladder, man.
I'll slap on the paste.
Stick it where they'll read it.
Shinde's wife makes good paste,
But his father's from Hell.
Islya's mother, oof!
What a tough bird.
I tried to sneak off
And stepped on a dog…
Even more noise.'

'Don't stick it near that window.'
                    'Why not?'
'His chick lives over there.
If everyone looks that side, he'll be screwed.'
'Islya, Islya, look here,
Should we stick one over his uniform?'
'Shh, keep it down.
That old man's here, painting one letter at a time.
He's a tightass.'

When the four of us return to four homes,
The poles on our shoulders set up an itch,
And the leaves on the trees begin to whisper.

'Islya re, tomorrow's a meeting.'
'To hell with it. I'm for a good sleep.'
'Sleep? If you're off to Hell,
We'll load you on this ladder,
And pack you off to the graveyard.'

'Look, Shinde, a sliver of moon.
Ghalib's ghazal haunts me:
"*Bekaar zindagi ne Islya ko nikamma kar diya*
Varna Islya bhi aadmi tha, ishq ke kaam aataa."'*
'Shut up, Islya, talk-talk-talk.'

'Hanmya, let's do one thing.'
  'Objection.'
'Let's take up a collection.'
  'Objection.'
'Let's get Islya married.'
  'Then, full support.'

---

* Surve riffs on Ghalib's famous sher:
Ishq ne, Ghalib, nikamma kar diya
Varna hum bhi aadmi the kaam ke.
(Love has destroyed Ghalib, ripped out my pith
For once I was a man to reckon with.)
Surve's character says:
This useless life has left me abused.
Or Islya was once a man Love might have used.

'A pretty little bride will come to my home
With shehnais playing.'

'How much the world has progressed
Right in front of our noses.
Behind us, the old men glare.
Which is why I say, Islya,
Get the old boys some spectacles.'
        'Idea!'

Just such a Brahma am I

Over my shoulder I toss
    The cosmic egg of creation,
And settle down to resolve
    The space-time equation.

Outside the door of my home,
    The world's pleasure gardens disport.
I yank at the reins of the sun
    And Ol' Sol pulls up short.

Great herds of cloud pachyderms
    Stand and wait on my whim.
With the nectar of the immortals,
    I fill my jar to the brim.

In my courtyard, urchin winds
    Dance and spin their tops.
The doors of heaven glint
    And sparkle with glittering drops.

With my brawny arm it is I
    Who steadies the sky when it's slipping.
And when it behaves badly,
    It is I who gives it a whipping.

Each mountain a mustard seed,
    Each mustard seed a mountain.
And both immanent in me,
    Both mine to contain.

Just such a Brahma am I,
    Lynchpin of earthly might.
A Brahma with no home
    That he can claim by right.

My entry in the logbook of my nation

Khrushchev, Kennedy, Nasser, et cetera, et cetera.
My name with theirs? No way.
So I turn twenty-five pages
and on page twenty-six,
I place a rose and begin.

My country, my country,
If indeed we belong to the dynasty of the sun,
Can we behave in a manner that befits the sun?

Today, I am neither happy nor sad.
I'm somewhere in between.
Perhaps we've both grown up, you and I.

You know, when I set out to come here,
The trees offered their kindly green shade,
Right up to the edge of the city.
The rivers shifted course,
The leaves took wing and flew above me,
The roads strode ahead of me.
One of them, a loquacious sort, said:
'If you don't know the way,
I'll show you,' but he went off,
Walking ahead of me.

My country, my country.
Your megacities that have grown out of little ones,
These cities whose doors open and close,
Flashing light and shade,
With villages at suck,
Until a rebel calf breaks the halter, breaks loose, breaks free.

These roads are veins,
This metropolis a thundering boiler.
This is our heart: yours and mine.
We bathe in delight.
It shines, this city: a constellation unto itself.
It shines, a diamond ring on your finger.
City by the Arabian Sea,
Have you ever looked at yourself?
I only say this because we belong
to the dynasty of the sun, remember?

This sky, consider this sky.
It needs a slap or two of paint.
The fireball of the sun?
Turn it to face the Bhilai furnaces.
Drain the sea: give it a pretty new name.
Break up the fields; reorder them in a neat row.
My country, we must always remember
What it takes to be called a country.

Before a bill goes to the Lok Sabha
It should flap in the muddy hand of the farmer.
It should be tested against mountain breeze,
Tree shade and the cloud-cool air.
It should go to the factory floor,
Be leaned against a lathe.
Let the workers discuss it at break time,
Even as they exchange their coupons for tea.
Let the unwanted words
Be remoulded in the furnace by hammer and tong.

Send it to the outskirts of the village,
Where cattle hides are being tanned.
Let some stitches be added there.

And

Bring it to the classes at the University,
Not wearing the Vice-Chancellor's scowl
But carrying with it the scent of a friend.

My country, my country,
Because of our membership in that dynasty of the sun,
I say,
If your elites only see women as sex toys, as egg-layers,
As bouquets at the florist,
As dolls, as bodies…
The shame should crush us all; it crushes me.

My country, know this:
We remember all this,
We store all this in our hearts
Like petrol.
And if one day we are stirred,
If our horses buck and stamp,
If we turn in a new direction
In search of a new light,
Do not call us ingrates.
For remember, my country, we too belong,
We too are stars in your sky.

Crows crowd city chowks

The crows have slipped away,
After crowding the city's central chowk.

They drip-dropped droppings onto the statues.
They flapped their wings, turned in circles,
And then sat tight.

Announcements were made.
Fatwas were issued.
And the speeches, oh the speeches.
From North to South, speech after speech.
With no authority vested in them,
They declared themselves the true swamis.

They set up a United Front,
Erected a tent, called a meeting.
'This is to inform the public at large…'
Shoulder to shoulder, they went on parade.

An elder crow took the oath,
Another crow made a speech on democracy.
A second crow made one on corruption.
A third thumped his drum about culture.
A fourth and so forth…

Next:
Dropping his broken body into a chair,
An ancient leader made a speech
That lasted a heroic hour-and-a-half.
Then they sang each other's praises.

Swooping, nose-diving, circling,
They rewrote the map of the city.

The cloud of their black wings
was to lay siege to Parliament.
They were to swoop down on the offerings
and indicate that the souls of the dead have taken flight.

They have all gone underground.
The crows of the city have melted away.

A chat with Mardhekar*

Were you at the mehfil, Mardhekar?
I looked for you everywhere.
You were nowhere to be seen.
Let's say it's not in your nature to mingle in such crowds.
But your poem was there,
Meeting and greeting people,
Saying, 'Everyone drinks this sweet winter.'†

I thought we'd meet there.
And after it was all over,
We could have sat on a kerb
In Girgaon or even Girangaon, wherever,
And talked about everything.
We could have uncovered the truth
Of all that the gods have brought to birth
Upon this earth.

---

* Bal Sitaram Mardhekar (1909–1956), poet and novelist, often described as the first modernist of Marathi poetry. He received the Sahitya Akademi award in 1956.

† This is a line from an iconic Mardhekar poem, '*Nhaalela Janu Garbawatichya*' (Like a pregnant woman stepping out of a bath), which is about winter in Bombay. The line is 'pitaat saare gōd hivaala'.

Leaning back on the unreliable pillar of poetry,
Your elbows resting on your knees,
Your head in your hands, I hear you saying with a sigh:
'Do something about this, please.'
I watch as your tired, dispirited tree
Heaves with grief, Mardhekar.
Even as the bastions of values crumble,
How did you maintain your concern for people?
What link did you see?
What held you?

Our predecessors,

Those out of Malgund,* were heavyweights.
Their mettle was tested.
We traced their words on our flags,
And yet they too had to line up
In the queue for seniority.
How dull we are, Mardhekar, how dull.
It took a hundred years to reach Malgund.
But those who went
Came back content
And returned to the struggle
For bread and rent.
The ants were back to the anthill.

---

* Malgund is home to Keshavsut (1866–1905) who Surve sees as an important moment in the history of writing in Marathi (see his introduction); and to a literary festival and many bookshops.

The grocer from Dehu[*] was bundled out long ago.
But let's talk about Ganpat, the modern-day grocer,[†] and
his journey.
He's sucked out the juice and spat out the cane a while ago.
He's built himself a two-storey house.
He talks up a storm on the floor of the Assembly.
He's got a brand new car outside his door.
He says: 'I will build a new NEPA[‡] factory.'
These are our ancestors.
They clean forgot to write about our valour.
What do you say to that, Mardhekar?

The academics too turned out to be cunning.
They bundle up your words and skim
The surface of your conflicts.
They graft the spiritual onto them.
Your people are rooted deep in the soil.
The academics talk only of the flowers and the leaves.

What is beautiful, Mardhekar, is true,
And what is true is revolutionary and dynamic.
What is impermanent changes, sure.
But the eternal changes too, Mardhekar.

---

* This refers to Sant Tukaram, the iconic seventeenth century poet-saint of Maharashtra.

† This is a reference to Mardhekar's poem '*Ganpat Vani*'.

‡ This was the first indigenous newsprint manufacturing unit in the country. It was originally floated by a private entrepreneur and taken over by the government in 1959.

Not that I need to tell you all this.
But it's what I discovered in my daily struggle.
When the human is erased, what is left?

It's a good thing I didn't meet you, Mardhekar,
A good thing.
For a poet's ego is enormous, they say.

Manifesto

In the name of this day,
In the name of this day's sorrows,
In the name of the hemisphere slowly emerging into light,
In the name of the needs of this day's creative urge,
    of every moment of waiting,
    of the ailments demanding surcease,
    of those pilgrims of the mind,
fluttering desperately to evade bullets.

Where the day must be leaning against a wall,
Where the closed gates of the city must be opening,
Where the rain is washing the city clean as a ship's freshly-
    scrubbed deck,
When a sheet of ice spreads itself over the village and
by the mellow light of a candle, an old priest says:
'He was born and the shepherds saw a bright new star.'

A cold front moves down from the North Pole;
The workers of Paris are hot,
Watching a flock of penguins.
In Capri, she rests on the bosom of her lover.
Perhaps the Thames descends into the Atlantic, heart
    thundering.

Perhaps Hamlet has run mad,
And perhaps a dark swollen cloud
Is heading steadily to Hindostan.

In the name of reality, toiling ceaselessly, her dreams
hanging on a peg,
In the name of the furnaces that are melting steel to shape
into minds,
In the name of the slender fingers limp with exhaustion
from plucking tea,
In the name of poetry, pregnant with intention, eager to
give birth and lay down her burden,
In the name of cosmic motions,
In the name of she who cuts the umbilicus by the flickering
light of an earthen lamp.

Comrades! The evening of this century has begun.
The new century is knocking at the door.
Even this one will go and settle down into the pages of
history.
It will demand an accounting of its achievements
—in the year 1917, 1937, 1947—
And all the numbers still to come.
Teachers will put these figures on the blackboard,
At most, use their canes to draw lines on the map.

But who can tell? The Moon grew more expensive in this century.
My soul became a horse drawing a buggy through the streets of Calcutta.
Enough. I too should change my grimy spectacles.
I too was born in this century.
I too shall have to account for myself.
How often I was entered as an asset into the Marwari's accounts!
How often my life teetered on the edge of bankruptcy!
How many cries resounded in the forests!
How many aeroplanes have roared overhead!
We just kept changing scripts, kept changing doors out of expediency,
Kept replacing the tiles that have been blown off.

Comrades! The evening of this century has just begun.
One atom bomb is all it will take to capsize our canoe.
In a blink, we will be full fathoms five.
Hiroshima at least grew flowers later.
But we...

Evening is falling.

I wander, carrying an unwritten existence with me.
I stop to read the signboards of tradition.
I find no one to call my own.
I move on.

A lamp. Another.
A hand moves swiftly lighting one lamp with another.
That's all the support there is.

Evening is falling.

I present my case.
Stuff and mount the words: 'I swear by God'.
I swear by myself.
I demand justice from you but only after
You have denuded the culture shop of all readymade clothes.
If I sit naked on the seat of judgement,
Will you tolerate it?
Will you accept me?

I watch as my selfhood sprouts wings.
The conch sounds through veins of steel.
I am truth; the earth is truth.
I am for everyone, this is also a truth.
For all of us.

Death dodders along, leaning on a stick.
The children drive it away, with stones
That topple his pyramid.

Religion: a sickly stray slinking through lanes and alleys.

Drop by drop, my blood drips
Between these two poles.

And Comrades, I keep watch
And I write this holding on to a newborn, explosive trajectory.

Get rid of these words, these statues.
They're static. I wrote this because
I wanted a new manifesto
To match the new mind.

Song of the mill

It's seven in the morning
The foghorn is yawning
The first shift's ready and set.
The wheels are turning
The spindles are burning
We'll dress the world with our sweat.

A nine-yard sari has to be spun
Only the bobbin just wants to have fun
And keeps the machine in red heat.
The breeze won't stop trying
To keep the fluff flying
The doffer must make split ends meet.

Our sweat is the fuel we burn
As the levers of Brahma we turn
To pour out a cascade of colour.
The skies give us blues
The fields their green hues
Our cloth makes the rainbow look duller.

With the season's turning
My field of cloth's burning
Chaitra pours down the heat.

Shravan's a-soaking
Winter fires need stoking
But Kabir never misses a beat.

This Chandrakala
Has the same colour
As the glint in a peacock's eye.
Paithanis, brocades
Thousands of shades
Roses bloom from chemical dye.

As the Kauravas court
The Princes disport
To Krishna she makes supplication.
Panchali's sari won't end
Thus does he defend
Her modesty from humiliation.

It is we who make wealth
For those thieves' good health:
The owners who amass much riches.
We've no money to eat
Hunger has us beat
Should we seal our stomach with stitches?

Butcher

'What are you writing, boy?'
'Nothing, Chacha, just pushing some words around.'
Dawood Chacha comes in,
takes off his fez,
wipes sweat from his neck, his chest,
takes a swig of Beechband
and sits down.
His crutch falls, spreadeagles next to him.

'Keep one thing in mind, kid.
It's all very well to write words.
It's tough to live by them.

'Take a look at my leg.
Your mother, Kashibai, she's my witness.
I'm a butcher, son, but
we don't cut any pregnant animals.

'So innerpendence came, Gandhi-style.
And Allah said: be merciful.
Our chawl folks? You never saw the like.
Such processions as we had,
your dad right in the middle of it.

'What was I saying?
Ah yes, one day at the butchery,
I had just skinned a goat, skewered it,
set it on the grill…
Suddenly, a shouting.

'I ran. I saw.
In the crowd, your Ammi.
"Cut her," said the Allah-hu-Akbarwallas.
"Over my dead body," I said.
They laughed at me.
"This one's turned out a right Hindu.
Cut this kaafir then,"
the Allah-hu-Akbarwallas shouted.
And we set to.
Oh, they beat me, they beat me good.
I saved my life. Lost my leg though.
Right or wrong, Kashibai?

'So son—
Human life? That's cheap.
Mutton? That's expensive.
Life is dark, son, dark.

'To live for words, you need heart enough.
And here we are: with snouts in the trough.'

Karl Marx

It was during my first strike
That I met Karl Marx.
Like this.

In the middle of the procession,
I was holding up his banner.
'Know who that is?' Janaki Akka asked.
'That's our Marxbaba.
Born in Germany.
Wrote sacks of books.
Buried in English soil.
Don't think he minds.
All soils are one, no,
To a sanyasi?
He also had four children
Like you.'
That's how I met Marx.
During my first strike.

Another day, at a meeting, I asked:
'What brought on this Depression?
What's the lineage of poverty?'
Again Marx said: 'Let me explain.'
And he talked and talked, like an express train.

I was listening to a gate speech one day.
'Now we are the heroes of history,' I said,
'And of all future biographies.'
At that he burst out laughing
And clapped the loudest.
Then he stepped up to me and
put his hand on my shoulder:
'Do you write poetry-shoetry?
Good, good.
I too loved Goethe.'

Stand firm

When I'm not there to eat
The rice you cook with so much love,
Know this: I'm in a meeting,
Planning a better tomorrow.
Don't wait for me.
Eat.

On a night drenched in stars,
When your young body thirsts
And I'm not there,
Know this: I'm in the thick of it,
Drawing up a new charter of demands.

Monsters may descend on you,
Thundering on the door.
They may raid the house.
They may take you away.
Don't you tremble. Not for a moment.

Stand firm.

Mumbai

From the Sahyadris he came to the City of Slog and
Tussle.
With a rag over his shoulder, he brought you the gift of
his muscle.

When he came and when he went only Aai could gauge.
One night, I was born, in a house bent with age.

On payday he went beserk, banging things about.
Aai cowered in a corner, waiting his rages out.

He'd grab me and hug me and toss me to the sky.
His laugh was wild but my cheeks knew the slaps could
also fly.

In his way, he loved us; but City, you had his heart.
In every month of his life, thirty days were your part.

Ever since I can recall, I took him his bhakri and pickle.
In that mill, I too was forged, as a blacksmith does a sickle.

I learned to string cotton, to fit spindle to socket just right.
And in good time, I learned to down tools to fight the
good fight.

He lay down his life in you, for you, City by the Sea.
To that very machine, the sickly super appointed me.

The sea is now an inkpot, overturned for a prank.
The child in me recalls those days, his heart dismal, dank.

Sinews taut in shining calves, the workers humped their loads.
In the water, I marked their tramp upon the weathered boards.

I am he, they are us, together we sculpt you, City.
Each day, we add our sweat and toil to the making of your beauty.

For ourselves, we live in the chawls of Hell, we clean the dirt of your streets.
Then the police come and we become, the dirt of your streets.

Evicted, we pick up the pieces and settle in the next gutter.
We scrape on, scrape by, in this rotten, rotting culture.

The next morning, we wake again, ready to take on the day.
We work, we toil, we burn, in the city's constant affray.

We wander through you, City, your ways a maze deployed.
Sometimes we're citizens, householders; sometimes the unemployed.

Until the moon gives up, goes down, these streets will be bright.
On either side, neon signposts flank the City of the Night.

The throngs move on, they churn, they drift as throngs must.
I move with them, directionless, a floating speck of dust.

Were I to seek direction, I know two ways to go:
One leads to the maw of the mill, the other to death's door.

Old friends who walked with me drift into the sarai of my mind.
They ask me to tell their stories; they form an orderly line.

How to describe you? You are iron, you are stone.
Even the flowers that fall from you can bruise the unwary bone.

You were the cornerstone on which was set the City by the Sea.
You have left indelible marks on Mumbai and on me.

You give me solace, courage in my lonely hours.
As the lights on the seashore offer company to the stars.

With my children on my shoulder, I set off on festive days.
The royal road is alive with flowers, my little ones also blaze.

Suddenly their balloons airlift me to a childhood space.
Baba striding on ahead, Aai scurrying to keep pace.

My children ask me, just as a smile breaks upon my face,
'Why these stone walls, Baba? Why do police guard this
place?'

The question slams my heart, a sledgehammer hits my
brain.
My throat chokes with rage. I might explode in pain.

My steps grow cautious, saving strength, as palanquin-
bearers learn.
I am struck dumb; I bring them home: they're all that I
could earn.

Sleep does not come that night. My eyes burn in the dark.
My soul splutters and sizzles, damp firewood to the spark.

My father wore out like sandalwood rubbed upon a stone.
What of my buds? Will darkness claim them for its own?

My heart is full to bursting. I yearn for catharsis.
These words don't work; my father too wrote inspiring
verses.

My university

I had no home, I had no kin, just the earth beneath my feet.
I curled up rough in front of shops; or slept free on the street.

I did not ask to be born; I took the life I got.
Through nights and days I realized, darkness was my lot.

I knew each pillar on each street; each word on each shop sign.
I've seen men being erased, when they messed up the bottomline.

Past colonies of high caste walls and ghettoes based on class,
I watched as carrion crows swooped down on a carcass.

In the ruins of a burned-out city, blasted by the pox,
Where tongas come and horses fall, I guarded the horse-shoe box.

'Get that rope. Hold it. Tight. Tight,' I said. 'Scared, you little shit?
You a brahmin's son? Too good for this? Ah-ha, yes. That's it.'

Horse-shoe Yakub's laugh thundered when a horse rose
from the ground.
'Tobacco for me, jalebis for you,' he said, and pushed the
next horse down.

The riots took him. Not my kin but I couldn't stop my
weeping.
I chanted the Milad Kalma as he went to the earth's
safe-keeping.

That very day I wrote on a blank page of my mind,
'Hé Narayana, this world strips men. Learn to read the
signs.'

I met men of every stripe: brothers, fathers, exploiters
some.
I seared my soul on a tarry griddle, baked by a relentless
sun.

The endless inventiveness of humankind impresses me.
With thirty-seven pages of my story done, how little I've
seen depresses me.

I've met no real men, that is sad. The self undiscovered?
Sadder.
What of it? I've stumbled too on the thirty-seven steps of
this ladder.

Life is babysmooth, soft and sleek, just like the cover of
a book.
Inside: words are limp carcasses, dangling from a butcher's
hook.

The meaning of life circles back to be locked in its own
book.
Memory wanders in gardens and beaches, a pensioner
with a blind look.

I see this, I ask: 'Hé Narayana, why this flaying?'
And I find I am the victim of a senseless slaying.

The past consumes me as a candle-flame gobbles its wax.
I am a soldier seeking the lost in a city ravaged by attacks.

I've read so many books; I've conned so many words.
Confronted with experience, every tome explodes.

I tried to befriend books, but, like us, they were rotten.
No worker's flair, no nurse's care, their gains were ill-
gotten.

We get by on a small stash of words, we take those beyond
the pale.
While suave words with barren hearts will live to tell the
tale.

This story lifts me gently as steam lifts a pot on the boil.
Yet I'm spent, as after an asthma attack, a lamp that has
no oil.

Why did Yakub have to die? Why put African Chacha
    in stocks?
Why was Chandra's only son picked clean by war's vulture
    flocks?

Chandra, mill super, neighbour, limps home with cotton-
    flecked hair.
Wisps of white cotton cloud hang from her here and there.

Unlettered, she bought the dailies which I read by
    candlelight.
'If we stand firm, how will they win?' she'd crow with
    delight.

She'd cut scraps from dozens of maps; she sought him in
    each one.
When she'd scoured the stations and barracks, she took
    me for her son.

Chandra dies too. I weep stone tears. My mind petrifies.
I sit on her steps as the sunlight does. To leave is to break
    off ties.

The white man's ships rock at anchor under the sky's
    blue dome.
We break our backs on those planks, carrying his loads
    back home.

'Pig!' 'Dog!' 'Bloody Indian!' Like bullets the curses whistle.
The white women's faces split open, mortars without pestles.

African Chacha raged, 'I won't work for the crude.'
I lit the chillum and I said, 'What will you do for food?'

His calves turned to stone as he filled rail car after car.
Then came the decisive day when the bosses went too far:

He ripped off his sweaty shirt and flew it from a crane.
It was a banner of the revolt brewing in my guru's brain.

'Long live our blood!' African Chacha roared and overturned the world.
We devoured his words, and along our nerves, a flood tide unfurled.

They came for him, they chained him up, they hauled the lion away.
His throat was choked, a tear broke free, 'My son,' he managed to say.

Where is my guru? In what cell? Why does he rot in jail?
I feel his hand upon my back. Where, how did we fail?

I was born into this world. I can't escape it yet.
It's what I have. It's harsh, it's real, I'll give as good as I get.

Mother

As the stars faded into the morning,
And the siren shrieked its shrill warning,
A procession of feet shuffled to the mill.
Aai's feet too, her eyes on us still.
'Don't fight,' she said, and to keep the peace,
She left us with two pice each.

On the eve of Dassehra, she took us all five
To the shrine, to see the Devi go live.
How we danced and sang through the whole fair!
How to tell of the fun we had there!
Pinwheels, spinwheels, balloons in herds,
We grew wings, we flew as birds.

One day, they heaved her onto a cart.
Her eyes were staring, blood at her mouth.
Salu, her companion, took us under her wing.
'Oh my babies,' she said, 'You poor things.'
We blinked as we looked for our mother,
We blinked as we looked for something.

That night we clung one to the other,
Seeking a mother's love from one another.
We knew now we had had nothing before.
Now we had nothing minus a mother.
We held back the tears, lips pressed tight,
Not one of us slept through the orphaning night.

When Nehru died

The houses were warming their backs
When the city went grey,
Then fig-purple.
Finally: darkness swallowing rubies.

The mills wore stone gowns.
They lit cheroots, and then,
With wet shirts tossed over
Their shoulders, they turned
To the coop.

'What happened, ay Sundre?'
'Don't fire up the incense today.
Didn't you hear? Nehru's gone.'
'Really? It's a holiday, then.'
Exhausted, the world fell into bed.

Forlorn, I walked on.
The roads were frightening.
I came upon a handcart puller,
Carrying light in paper.

'Where are you taking that light?'
'Come on, sir!
Up ahead the darkness bares its teeth.'
All this when Nehru died.

Put your own name down, Masthur*

Write, Masthur.
Put your own name down.

I'll tell you the truth
With Mari Aai for witness.
You write.
Look at the rat nests in his hair, Masthur.
The gift of the gods, yes, the gods.†

Masthur, the earth is upturned,
Fertile, ready.
But if there's no plough,
        if there's no seed,
What will come out?
Will anything sprout?

---

* Masthur began its life as 'Master', the English word. But in Marathi, it acquired all kinds of secondary meanings, so that you may address anyone in authority—such as a bus conductor on a Mumbai bus—as 'Masthur'. In the voice of this sex worker, it is respectful and ironic and I could not put in another word for fear of losing her voice entirely.

† Hair that is tangled or tousled is often considered to be a message from the Goddess, demanding her own or marking the child out as hers. In *Strike a Blow to Change the World* (Speaking Tiger, 2018), Eknath Awad talks about his father's matted locks as being Mari Aai's trees, a sign of her favour.

So how will it do, then,
To put my name as his father?
How will it do to say
That the boy has no father?

One day, my belly dropped.
Just like that.
No midwife, no nothing.
First, there was fear.
But soon there was love.

No.
Not the name of a god,
It has to be a man's name.
What's God got to do with this?
It was a man who did this.
A man filled my pot.
So your name, Masthur.
Put your name down.

Don't ask my caste.
We're not the one-man kind of woman.
Not the kind of woman you marry.
That's not our lot.

Touch his feet, boy.
Go on, touch them.
Fall at his feet.
Only do this much, Masthur:
Put your own name down.

My field on the hill

That field of mine, up on a hill,
How long must I weed it?
How many years must I kill,
Knocking myself out to feed it?

How long must I climb and crawl
With firewood on my head?
How much water do I haul
For one lousy crust of bread?

How long must my baby scream,
Scream and scream alone?
His mama's dugs they burst with milk,
But she can't stay at home.

Every year we plough the earth
Till the corn gilds the fields.
But then the shitbag moneylender
Grabs what our work yields.

Prices soar and ruin looms,
I feel the noose's bite.
What do I pay for? This or that?
How long must we fight?

This life we live brings no relief.
They take the crops we've grown.
They leave us naked, shivering, wet.
How long can we go on?

We must guard each home, each hearth,
For life itself to blossom forth.
We must redraw the face of the earth,
Must smash the fetters of our birth.

We must break free, we must cut loose,
We must slip out of the hangman's noose.
Go tell it across the face of the land.
On my backbreaking hill, I make my stand.
A flag of unity in my hand.

Usman Ali

A well-built man, a strapping man,
His skin aglow with a coppery tan.
In his manner,
A Deccan swagger,
A tang of old Hyderabad.
His brawny shoulders rock hard,
His feet tough with roots,
        not boots.
Eleven children he had
From two wives.
He'd joke: 'That's my tribe.'

'So we came back from the War in 1946.*
We were on board a ship; we mutinied,
Declared ourselves against the British,
Got ready to die. We flew all three flags.
The people came, oh yes, the people came.

---

* Some of the ratings of the Royal Indian Navy mutinied in February 1946. For more details, I recommend, B.C. Dutt, *Mutiny of the Innocents*, reissued recently. Dutt was one of the sailors who took part in the Mutiny. Usman Ali taking a job as a chaprasi in the Municipality points to how the Indian Navy did not reinstate these sailors who had mutinied for patriotic reasons, seeing themselves as part of the Independence movement. Dutt himself became a journalist with the *Free Press Journal.*

But not one leader.
We didn't lose, no,
But it felt like losing.
Afterwards, I got a job in the Municipality
As a chaprasi.'

He broke off suddenly.
'Go on up—it's that Bhendi Bazaar School.
You'll meet the top bosses.
Tell them Usman Ali sends greetings.
Add your own and hurry back.'

When I returned, Usman Ali
Took up where he had left off.
'I have two wives.
One does the housewifery,
The other works in hosiery.
These women are smart as hell.
They look after me
And my tribe as well.

'The eldest boy sells kites
On the beach at Chowpatty.
When work's done, I teach
The elders the Urdu primer.
When you've delivered those letters
And your beat is done, we'll go home.
Have a bite to eat.
You will eat at a Muslim home?

You're afraid of a Muslim area?
Men are the same everywhere, you louse.
If you're united at work
You'll be united at home too.
I learned that on the high seas.'

Usman Ali, sailor of the seven seas,
Usman Ali, at prayer, at his ease,
All through '46 and its worries,
His mat by his side, hankie on his head,
The azaan sounds, prayers to be said,
The world faded into the distance.
For Usman Ali would be on his knees.
Come what may,
He would pray.

I'd cover for him if he were called,
I'd answer the boss if the bell tolled.
Usman Ali, father of eleven,
Usman Ali, freedom fighter, vintage '47,
Usman Ali, a friend who knew,
How to keep his faith
And his friendship too.

Many months passed us by,
No sign of Usman Ali?
I hadn't seen him around.
Thought I'd run him to ground.
When the letters were done,

I went to his door.
I couldn't believe what I saw.
A white-haired Usman Ali,
A broken Usman Ali.

'Come in, come in.
Rasool, get your Uncle a cup of tea.'
I sat down. 'In the last
Four months, I've buried eleven
Of my family. Some were taken
In the riots here, some in Hyderabad.
I've been running from grave to grave.

'My parents died, their hearts were broken.
My brother was also taken.
One of my wives died,
Our children too.
Now I've lost heart. I think
I'll sell this room, pay my debts
And go home to dangle my legs
In a grave. But at least it will be
A grave in my native land.
Tell everyone, Usman Ali says:
Khuda hafiz.'

What I heard
Left me no words.
What could I say?
I heard words from another day:

'We didn't lose, no,
But it felt like losing.'
Khuda hafiz, Usman Ali.
God keep you, Usman Ali.
Khuda hafiz.

TRANSLATOR'S ACKNOWLEDGEMENTS

It takes a little village for me to translate anything and poetry is a demanding form.

So my thanks go out to many people.

To Shanta Gokhale whose imprimatur I sought and received when first I thought to translate.

To Neela Bhagwat, the first filter of this translation.

To my personal assistant Santosh Thorat who helped with much of the first attempts.

And as always to Ravi Singh, whose constant support gives me courage.

ALSO FROM SPEAKING TIGER

MY LIFE IS A SONG

Gaddar's Anthems for the Revolution

Translated and with an Introduction by
Vasanth Kannabiran

Gaddar, poet, singer, revolutionary, is among the most well known of the creative minds associated with people's resistance movements in India. Born Gummadi Vittal Rao in 1947, in Tupran village of Medak district in what is now Telangana, Gaddar became an activist in his youth after dropping out of engineering college due to poverty. With a gift for singing and song-writing, he travelled the road—for some time underground—reaching lakhs of people with his music, and became the cultural face of 'rebellion', the literal meaning of his *nom de guerre.*

Gaddar's compositions are unpretentious, easily accessible to the peasant and labourer. But they aren't mere entertainment. They are weapons of the weak. When they speak of an unlettered peasant they also expose the system that swindles him. If they poke fun at the schooling the people receive, they also tell them what true education consists of. When they depict a mother's longing for her dead children, they also talk of her resolve for retribution.

Of the thousands of songs Gaddar performed, only a few were ever recorded in print. *My Life Is a Song* brings together, for the first time in English translation, twenty-three representative songs, selected by his friend and fellow traveller, Vasanth Kannabiran. Translated from the original Telugu with an eye to Gaddar's unique style and delivery, this selection takes the extraordinary 'anthems' of one of India's greatest singer-poets—and a living legend of revolutionary thought—to a wider audience.